9.22
Springar.

BLACK BIBLICAL STUDIES

An Anthology of

Charles B. Copher

Biblical and Theological Issues on The Black Presence in the Bible

D0922484

BLACK LIGHT FELLOWSHIP
Chicago, Illinois

BLACK BIBLICAL STUDIES
An Anthology of Charles B. Copher
Biblical and Theological Issues on The Black Presence in the Bible

Copyright © 1993 Charles B. Copher

Publisher: **Black Light Fellowship**

First Edition 1993
First Printing 1993

Cover Design: IFE DESIGNS & ASSOCIATES, *Philadelphia, PA*

Black Light Fellowship
128 S. Paulina St. · Chicago, IL 60612
Post Office Box 5369 · Chicago, IL 60680
312.563.0081

ISBN: 0-933176-38-4

Library of Congress Catalog Card Number: 92-43566

Library of Congress Cataloging-in-Publication Data

Copher, Charles B., date.
    Black biblical studies : biblical and theological issues on the Black presence in the Bible : an anthology of Charles B. Copher.
        p.   cm.
    Includes bibliographical references.
    Contents: Perspectives and questions -- The Black man in the Biblical world -- Blacks and Jews in historical interaction -- Egypt and Ethiopia in the Old Testament -- African Americans and Biblical hermeneutics -- Biblical characters, events, places, and images remembered and celebrated in Black worship -- Three thousand years of Biblical interpretation with reference to Black peoples -- Racial myths and Biblical scholarship -- The Bible and the African experience.
        ISBN 0-933176-38-4 :
        1. Blacks in the Bible. 2. Bible--Criticism, interpretation, etc.
    I. Title.
BS680.B48C67 1993
220.8'30596--dc20   92-43566

Manufactured in the United States of America.
98 97 96 95 94 93
10 9 8 7 6 5 4 3 2 1

#2172622

Dedication

To the institutions and organizations herein recognized, to the seminary students who have participated with me in classes and seminars on the "Black Presence in the Bible" since 1969, and to the numerous other persons, clergy and lay, members of various churches, public school administrative and faculty personnel, who have attended my lectures on the subject over the past two decades, this volume is dedicated.

Table of Contents

Preface

In the course of my presentation of lectures on the subject "Black Peoples and Personalities in and of the Bible," several individuals and groups have requested copies of articles, lectures and papers that I have written during the past twenty-five years. It now appears that a good way to respond to the requests is through a collection of some of the writings into a book. This I have done in the present volume by bringing together a few of the writings as they for the most part have been published in journals and anthologies. Two have not heretofore appeared in print.

It is to be noted that the entries go back to 1970 and continue through the summer of 1988. They appear as they were first printed or as I first prepared them except where there were errors or omissions in the printed text, especially in a few footnotes. No attempt has been made to bring any of them up-to-date nor to revise although some of them could very well undergo such treatment. (Also, the articles have undergone only slight grammatical editorial revisions.) Development in my thought across the years may be detected.

An apology for duplications and repetitions of content among some of the chapters is required, and I readily offer it: what now appear as chapters in a book were not originally written as such. All but two were produced upon assignment or by specific request, for a specific occasion, and more than one request was made for much the same content.

I offer words of thanks to those who have expressed an interest in such a collection as this, and to those who have made production of the volume possible. In the first category especially are members and friends of numerous churches and other community organizations together with their leaders who have sponsored me in lecture series on *two or more* occasions across the years.

Outstanding among these are the following: Atlanta Public Schools, African and African American Curriculum Infusion Project, Mrs. Gladys Tyman, Coordinator; Bethlehem United Methodist Church, Atlanta, during the pastorates of the Reverends Elisha Norwood, Frederick R. Gray, and Earl F.

Dabney; Chapel of Christian Love Baptist Church, Atlanta, the Reverend James A. Milner, Pastor; Grace Covenant Baptist Church, Atlanta, the Reverend Charles L. Stokes, Pastor; Greater Travelers Rest Baptist Church, Decatur Georgia, the Reverend Hubert T. Shepherd, Pastor; Gulfside Assembly Elderhostel, Waveland, Mississippi, Mrs. Nora S. Kellogg, Coordinator; Hillside International Truth Center, Atlanta, the Reverend Barbara Lewis King, Founder and Chief Minister; Lincoln Memorial United Methodist Church, Buffalo, New York, the Reverend Melba V. Chaney, Pastor; Metropolitan Missionary Baptist Church, Kansas City, Missouri, the Reverend Wallace S. Hartsfield, Sr., Pastor; Mount Ephraim Baptist Church, Atlanta, the Reverend R.L. White, Senior Pastor; Office For Black Catholic Ministry, Archdiocese of Atlanta, Ms. Rhonwyn Rogers, Director; Quality Living Services For Senior Citizens, Atlanta, Ms. Irene M. Richardson, Director; Springfield Missionary Baptist Church, Atlanta, the Reverend Arthur Carson, Jr., Pastor; St. Luke United Methodist Church, Dallas Texas, the Reverend Zan W. Holmes, Jr., Senior Pastor; St. Stephen's Church of God In Christ Ministries, San Diego, California, Bishop George D. McKinney, Founder and Senior Pastor; Turner Chapel A.M.E. Church, Marietta, Georgia, the Reverend Kenneth Marcus, Pastor; Wesley Chapel United Methodist Church, Decatur, Georgia, the Reverend Leon Hollinshed, Pastor; West Hunter Street Baptist Church, Atlanta, the late Reverend Ralph D. Abernathy, Senior Pastor; Zion Baptist Church, Marietta, Georgia, the late Reverend Robert L. Johnson, Pastor; and the Black Light Fellowship, Chicago, the Reverend Walter A. McCray, Founder and Director.

In the second category belong the present editors of the journals in which the entries first appeared in print who have granted permission to reprint. These are Dr. Gayraud Wilmore, *The Journal of The Interdenominational Theological Center*, Atlanta; Ms. Gail Buchwalter King, *Theological Education,* Pittsburgh; and Dr. Ivan Van Sertima, *Journal of African Civilizations,* New Brunswick, New Jersey. Next in order are my colleagues in Area I, Biblical Studies and Languages, the Interdenominational Theological Center, who provided a grant from their share of the Faculty Development Fund to assist with expenses of typing. Here also belongs Ms. Bernice Norman who with patience and love bore with me as she typed several drafts of the entries until they were ready for the editor-publisher.

Finally, in both categories belongs the Reverend Walter A. McCray, Founder and Director of the Black Light Fellowship,

Chicago.　He above all others has enabled me to publish the entries as they herein appear.　Not only did he encourage me to go ahead with the project; he and his organization have provided for all the processes that lead to and end in publication, distribution, and marketing. Indeed, without the Reverend　Mr. McCray the volume would not have been possible.　I can never repay the debt of gratitude I owe him and his coworkers.

Charles B. Copher
Atlanta, Georgia

BLACK
BIBLICAL
STUDIES

An Anthology of

Charles B. Copher

Biblical and Theological Issues on
The Black Presence in the Bible

Introduction

The several chapters of this book are held together by a common thread: each one and all represent biblical studies done from a Black perspective. However, on another hand, the author hopes that the chapters represent biblical studies done not from a Black but a universal, wholly objective position. Since a wholly objective position seems impossible among humans, then the author prays that what he has written is at least more universal than writings produced by all but a very, very few White authors in the fields of biblical studies.

Chapter one[1] was prepared as a paper to be read at a conference on "The Black Religious Experience and Theological Education" held February 20-23, 1970, at the School of Religion, Howard University, Washington, D.C. The author was assigned the topic, and being only newly introduced to the Black Awareness Movement, did not feel qualified to deal with the subject. What appears here is an initial, feeble attempt or essay. In it I set forth what appeared to me at the time a rationale for including the Black religious experience in the curricula of all Christian theological seminaries, not just Black ones, and offered suggestions as to how to go about the task of inclusion with special reference to biblical studies. Much to my pleasant surprise, favorable references to my rationale have been made in later years by Charles Shelby Rooks who as "chairman" of the special committee of the American Association of Theological Schools that sponsored the conference assigned the topic to me, and by Grant S. Shockley in one of his books.[2]

---

1. Reprinted with permission of *Theological Education*, in which it was first published, 6, no. 3 (Spring 1970): 181-188.

2. Charles Shelby Rooks, *Rainbows and Reality: Selected Writings of the Author* (Atlanta, Georgia: The ITC Press, 1985), Vol. 1 of *Black Church Scholars Series*, 153; *Revolution in Zion: Reshaping African American Ministry, 1960-1974* (New York: The Pilgrim Press, 1990), 101 f. Grant S. Schockley, General Ed., *Heritage & Hope: The African American Presence in United Methodism* (Nashville: Abingdon Press, 1991), 250.

Chapter two[3] is only the first part of what was to be an extensive essay on the presence of Black peoples within the biblical world. It was written in response to my discovery that some very important schools of White biblical interpretation had excluded Blacks, especially so-called "Negroes", from the biblical world and thus also from the Bible. The chapter proceeds to determine the presence or absence of Blacks upon the basis of several categories of evidence, and reports findings where the categories are applied to Egypt and to the country of Cush (ancient Ethiopia) in Africa. The categories of evidence dealt with are archaeological data, including written records, paintings, statuary, and skeletal remains; and modern historical works. It was first published as a contributory article in *The Journal of The Interdenominational Theological Center* 1, no. 2 (Spring 1974): 7-16.

Chapter three[4] was rather hastily prepared at the request of C. Eric Lincoln as a paper to be read at the National Consultation on Black-Jewish Relations held at Fisk University June 9-12, 1974, and sponsored jointly by Fisk University and the Interreligious Affairs Department of the American Jewish Committee. Although prepared upon short notice it rests upon research in which I had been engaged over the five previous years. It proceeds from a thesis that I had developed upon completion of the research begun in what is now chapter two of this book. The thesis is that upon the basis of American definitions of Black when applied to peoples in an ethnic or racial sense, definitions such as literally black, Negroid features, genealogical (one drop of African Negro blood), etc., the *Old Hamite View* is true. This old Hamite View is based upon the "Table of Peoples" in the tenth chapter of Genesis and regards the descendants of Ham therein listed (Cushite/Ethiopians, Mizraimites/Egyptians, Phutites, and Canaanites) as black. Further, that the ancient Elamites, Sumerians, and even Hebrews-Israelites-Judahites-Jews were also black as were the Hamites. In rapid succession the chapter presents relationships between Jews and their antecedent peoples and the other Blacks as they occurred in chronological order in the Old and New Testaments, beginning with Abraham and ending with the early Christians.

----

3. Reprinted with permission of *The Journal of The Interdenominational Theological Center.*

4. Reprinted with permission of *The Journal of The Interdenominational Theological Center.*

The paper was first printed in *The Journal of The Interdenominational Theological Center,* 3, No. 1 (Fall 1975):9-16. Later it was published in *African Presence in Early Asia,* Incorporating *Journal of African Civilizations,* 7, no. 1 (April 1985, Revised Edition 1988): 179-186, Ivan Van Sertima and Runoko Rashidi, editors. New Brunswick, New Jersey: Transaction Books.

Chapter four[5] was done as a paper requested by the Bennu Study Group of Atlanta for presentation at the Nile Valley Conference held in the Martin Luther King International Chapel, Morehouse College, September 26-30, 1984. It is related to Chapters two and three, dealing as it does with two Hamitic (Black) nations of the biblical world on one hand, and with relationships between Jews and the two Hamitic nations as they appear in the Old Testament on the other hand. An analysis of the number of references to the two nations is made along with particular bodies of literature in which the references are presented as is a conclusion that by far the references are of a negative nature.

The paper was published in *Nile Valley Civilizations* (Proceedings of The Nile Valley Conference, Atlanta, September 26-30, 1984), Incorporating *Journal of African Civilizations,* 6, no. 2 (November 1984): 163-178.

"African Americans and Biblical Hermeneutics" which appears as chapter 5, is a previously unpublished paper prepared at the request of Dr. John W. Waters, Professor of Old Testament Studies in the Interdenominational Theological Center, Atlanta, Georgia, and Dr. Thomas Hoyt, Professor of Biblical Studies, Hartford Seminary, Hartford, Connecticut, for presentation at the Black Biblical Studies Consultation, Society of Biblical Literature, annual meeting, December 8, 1984.

It presents the views of some Black authorities on the subject, and was later distributed among a group of Black scholars who represented a continuation of the Consultation of 1984, and who produced the book *Stony The Road We Trod,* edited by Dr. Cain H. Felder, 1991. Perhaps its significance lies in its being the first of papers on the subject among the particular group of scholars, as well as its informative contents compiled by one who already was in his sixth year of retirement and not active in the field of biblical studies.

----

5. Reprinted with permission.

Chapter six[6] originally was a paper prepared by request for presentation before a "Consultation on the Black Christian Worship Experience" sponsored by the Interdenominational Theological Center, November 21-23, 1985. Along with other papers, and solicited articles, it was published in the *Journal* of the Center, Volume XIV (Fall 1986, Spring 1987). It consists of a report of an investigation into five hundred and fifty Spirituals, two hundred and fifty Gospel Songs, fifty "Tindley" and similar Black Gospel Hymns, three hundred sermons, and twenty-five prayers with respect to references to biblical characters, events, places, and images that are employed in Black Christian worship.

Chapter seven[7] was prepared as a lecture for the Charles B.Copher lecture series in the Interdenominational Theological Center, 1987; and was presented a second time at the Howard University School of Divinity during the 1987-88 school year as the Jesse Herman Holmes Memorial Lecture.

It traces interpretation of the Bible with reference to Black peoples beginning with interpretation within the Bible itself and continues with interpretation among Jews and Gentiles, including Blacks, through the centuries during which the Bible in some form has existed.

More specifically, the chapter demonstrates that there is no curse upon Ham in the original biblical text of Genesis, chapter nine, but upon Canaan, one of Ham's sons; that there is no reference in the original texts to anyone having been turned black, including texts that deal with Cain; and the myths about the blackness of Cain, Ham, and Canaan originated with *interpretations* of the Bible by ancient rabbis, then spread among Muslims and Christians who added to the original stock of myths.

Published initially in *The Journal of The Interdenominational Theological Center,* 13, No. 2 (Spring 1986): 225-246, it was reprinted in *African American Religious Studies: An Interdisciplinary Anthology,* edited by Gayraud Wilmore (Durham, North Carolina: Duke University Press, 1989) 105-128.

Chapter eight, "Racial Myths and Biblical Scholarship," was done upon request as a paper for presentation at the March 1988 meeting of the Atlanta Old Testament Consortium which is comprised of professors of Old Testament Studies and Bible Majors in Candler School of Theology, Columbia Theological

---

6. Reprinted with permission.

7. Reprinted with permission.

Seminary, and the Interdenominational Theological Center. It presents examples of scholarly biblical interpretation that have employed myths with reference to Black peoples from the times of ancient Jewish rabbis unto today among Euro-American authorities. Thus the chapter deals more specifically than chapter seven with some matters, and indicates some myths that are used. It has not been previously published; and although it was prepared for an academic audience hopefully it can easily be understood by ordinary lay readers.

Chapter nine[8] was prepared upon request and read as a paper before the First Pan African Christian Church Consultation held July 17-23, 1988 at the Interdenominational Theological Center. It deals with references to Africa and its people in the Bible as they are interrelated with the Jews and their antecedent peoples (Hebrews-Israelites-Judahites) during the whole of the biblical historical period, 2000 B.C.-A.D. 100, in chronological order.

The content differs from that of chapter three in two main respects: it treats of Blacks in Africa rather than in the biblical world; and it represents development in the author's thought over the period of fourteen years which is the time between the dates of the two chapters. It was published, along with other papers and addresses of the Conference, in *The Journal of The Interdenominational Theological Center* 16, Nos. 1 and 2 (Fall 1988/Spring 1989): 32-50.

----
8. Reprinted with permission.

BLACK
BIBLICAL
STUDIES

An Anthology of
Charles B. Copher

Chapter 1

Perspectives and Questions: The Black Religious Experience and Biblical Studies

According to my understanding of this conference, there is a thesis which defines its nature and purpose. That thesis is: "The black religious experience should be included in the curriculums of all Christian theological seminaries." Beneath this thesis, supporting it and raising it up for serious, favorable consideration is a rationale. This rationale consists of at least five elements with varying degrees of weight, and which, although they are distinct, are closely interrelated. They may be distinguished as follows:

(1) The discovery and reclamation of a Black heritage that has been lost, unrecognized, or ignored as an entity of little or no value;

(2) The development of a sense of dignity and worth, and of pride in the Black heritage on the part of Black people;

(3) The increase of knowledge and the development of skills that will free Black people from oppression and dehumanization, and enable them to survive in an unjust society;

(4) The informing of White people of the Black heritage toward the end of changing attitudes

for the better, and of liberating White people from false notions; and,

(5) The investigation and analysis of the Black religious experience toward the end of discerning its liberating and life-sustaining aspects for the benefit of both Black people and White people.

One of the matters to be dealt with in this conference—in the light of the thesis and the rationale underlying it, is the subject that has been assigned to me for development: "Perspectives and Questions: The Black Religious Experience and Biblical Studies." Inasmuch as I was given the privilege of speaking "in my own way," I accepted the responsibility and here present the matter as I see it today. I confess ignorance at many points and limited vision. And at the very outset I find myself faced with serious difficulties. I find it necessary to clarify and define phrases and terms, aware that my clarifications and definitions may run counter to what others may have in mind.

In my position, particularly that of a dean in a predominantly Black theological institution which is situated in the midst of a predominantly Black university center, with still another Black cultural institution nearby, and as a member of a Black community, my attention is called to several perspectives daily. These perspectives are of different kinds, both with respect to the Black religious experience on one hand and theological education on the other. By that statement I mean that there is brought home to me the fact that several, not one, meanings accrue to the phrase "Black religious experience." Further, I mean that in regard to the phrase (whatever its meaning) as it has to do with theological education, there is more than one point of view. And these points of view represent different opinions about what should constitute theological education, particularly for Black students. Thus not only are there perspectives with reference to the meaning of the Black religious experience, there are also perspectives with respect to what properly does or does not constitute theological education.

However, the matter of perspectives with reference to theological studies goes further. It arises at the point of where content and scope of curriculums, courses and experiences are considered in an institution devoted to theological education. And to be sure, differences of opinion exist at this very point. Suffice it to say that what may be appropriate for a theological seminary which is part of a large university complex may or may not be appropriate for one that is unrelated or that is a small one.

The matter of various perspectives, then, is one that requires clarification and definition. From my own point of view at this present time, the matter in question is not one of perspectives; rather, it is one of a perspective. My statement of what that one perspective is must await clarification and definition of two other entities beforehand. These are the phrases "theological education" and "Black religious experience."

The meaning of theological education I find within the context of this conference; namely, a meeting of persons who represent primarily Christian theological seminaries, with emphasis on Christian and theological nature—however theology is to be defined and related to life in society.

Within the context of this conference the phrase "Black religious experience," it seems to me, has a limited meaning. It refers not to Black religious experience in general. To the contrary, it refers specifically to the religious experience of Black Christians as that experience has occurred and still takes place. Moreover, it has to do specifically with the religious experience of Black people resident particularly on the North American continent, Black people who are Afro-Americans.

The view of a Christian theological seminary as representing the Christian faith and commitment to that faith on the part of those who make up its life, together with the definition of Black religious experience, provides us with five axioms, so to speak, with regard to biblical studies.

(1) The Bible is the Scriptures, the source book directly or indirectly of the Black as well as of the White religious experience.

(2) The revelation of God recorded in the Scriptures is valid.

(3) Study of the Bible must ever be a part of the basic "body of divinity" in a theological curriculum.

(4) The Bible must be studied and interpreted according to its objective context—in keeping with sound methods, and in such a manner that study and interpretation contribute to the liberation of oppressed peoples (with special reference to Black people) from positions of indignity, dehumanization in an oppressive and destructive society; i.e., the Bible must be studied

and interpreted from a Black perspective as well as from a White one.

(5) Bible study and interpretation must lead eventually to a theology which recognizes and is expressive of the experiences of Afro-Americans in their actual existential situation of oppression.

What now is the one perspective in regard to the Afro-American religious experience as it relates to biblical studies—in the light of the rationale, the Christian theological institution, and the axioms? It is none other than that point of view inherent in the opening statement of this document: the Afro-American Christian experience should be recognized and incorporated in biblical studies. Or, to state the matter otherwise, biblical studies should take cognizance of and be related to the Black religious experience as herein defined.

The question now arises, "How to perform the task?" In reply, biblical studies may be "blackenized" or related to the Black religious experience in two ways: first, by the enrichment of courses that are already in the curriculum; second, by the addition of "Black courses" to the already existing curriculum.

ENRICHMENT OF EXISTING COURSES

The manner in which biblical studies may be related to the Black religious experience by enrichment of already existing courses may be illustrated in the instance of biblical history and related fields such as geography and archaeology. In this regard there exists not only possibilities for adding content; there is an already existent content within the biblical books themselves. Among some who in times gone by and some who still today regard the first eleven chapters of Genesis as factual history, taking Noah and his sons literally to be the progenitors of the races of mankind, Ham and his descendants were and are taken to be Black. Thus the presence of Black people in the biblical record is asserted without hesitation. Interesting it is to note, however, that many of such biblical interpreters regarded that Black presence to represent inferiority in every sense. No matter how high the degree of culture attained by Black peoples in the Bible it was depreciated. What is more, as most of us here know, the Bible, especially such passages as the so-called curse of Ham and the Genesis genealogical tables, was used to justify the enslavement of Black people. Additionally, law and order were provided the institution of Black slavery through the use of biblical passages. And still today many of the biblical passages that were employed to justify slavery are used to relate the Black man to, and keep him in, an inferior position within American society.

Furthermore, despite the fact that many White Christians moved away from the old noncritical methods of biblical interpretation, the results of the methods, the dehumanization of Black people, continue. On another hand, however, when White critical interpreters ceased to regard the lists and accounts of Ham and his descendants with reference to Black peoples they went, or so it appears, to another extreme. They lost sight of the possibility that at least some of the peoples in the Hamite genealogy might be Black. It is as if they came to regard them all as White, then at the same time developed a sense of appreciation for their cultures such as had not been true before.

The truth of the matter is that, depending on one's definition of Black, some of these peoples were either Black outright or had a large element of Black people within the overall population. And this holds true not only for some of the so-called Hamites; it holds true also for some so-called Semites, particularly the early Hebrews, and possibly for still others as well. All this is with reference to peoples who figure in biblical history through many periods and who appear at numerous places within the corpus of biblical literature. That these people were Black should be noted in the content of biblical history and such related studies as geography, archaeology, etc. To be more specific, we may take special note of the ancient Egyptians, Nubians, Ethiopians-Cushites, and lastly, of the Hebrews themselves.

Concerning the ancient Egyptians, archaeological remains indicate the presence of Black persons of all classes from Pharaohs to slaves. Monuments depict Black Pharaohs, and literature makes reference to Black groups, individual members of which even as slaves rose to high positions. Some present-day estimates consider the Black element to have constituted as much as one third the total Egyptian population.

Within the Old Testament itself Egyptians as Egyptians play a significant part from the beginnings of the history of Israel through the fall of the two kingdoms of Israel and Judah, and even into the Persian period. They appear over and over again in the prophetic books. And their influence on the Wisdom literature of the Old Testament and even on Hebrew religion is recognized. Egyptians under Nubian, Ethiopian-Cushite dynasties figured prominently in Israelite-Judean affairs particularly during the latter half of the eighth and the first part of the seventh century B.C.

Turning to the ancient Hebrew-Israelites, at least that group which was in Egypt had a Black element in it. A mixed multitude is reported to have accompanied the Hebrews in their departure from Egypt on the occasion of the Exodus, and according to sound authority members of that multitude were Black. Moses himself is reported to have married a Cushite woman, a Black wife. And today one need not wonder at the fact that the present population of Israel is as mixed in color as are the Black people in the United States of North America.

Apart from considerations of the extent of blackness among the ancient Hebrews, however, there is the established fact of Black persons living among them who are designated specifically as being black over against lighter shades of color. There are for instance, in addition to Moses' Cushite wife, the Cushite in the story of Absalom's revolt (I Samuel 18); Cushi, the father of the prophet Zephaniah who appears to have been a member of the royal Davidic family; and Ebed-Melech the eunuch who possibly as a government official came to the rescue of Jeremiah. And in the New Testament there is the Ethiopian eunuch who was converted to the Christian faith by Philip; and Symeon, called Niger, who was among the prophets and teachers in the church at Antioch (Acts 13:1).

The point of all this is that course content can be enriched by taking note of the Black presence in the Bible for whatever the records may be worth.

Another way whereby content of existing courses may be related to Black experience can be illustrated by a course such as Old Testament Introduction. References to Black persons and peoples as such appear primarily in the literature of the Old Testament. But there is a sense in which some parts of the literature may be viewed as the product of Black hands. Cushite in Hebrew refers to a person of Black color, and at least two persons in the Old Testament, Black in color, may be regarded as having produced writings that appear in the literary corpus. There is, first of all, the book of Zephaniah, the prophet previously mentioned. Secondly, there is the Cushite who appears along with Ahimaaz as a reporter to King David of Absalom's death. Biblical scholars raise a question with respect to the author of the large body of literature in which the narrative of Absalom's revolt occurs, the so-called Court History of David. Whoever he was, the author is regarded as the father of objective, factual, historical writing. And the only answers given as to his identity are based upon conjecture. Thus three persons who were close to the events are variously named as possible authors, but never the Cushite. Yet for the very same reasons given for the others the Cushite could have been the author just as well. It all depends on whether or not one can do Introduction in the Old Testament from a Black perspective.

Finally, with respect to the enrichment of the content of existing courses, a word may be said about biblical interpretation. If it is to be relevant, particularly for Black seminarians, it must be done from a Black as well as from a White perspective, and must relate the biblical word to the lives of Black people in their present situation, so that today among them the word becomes life. What is more, any course in biblical interpretation which deals with the history of the subject cannot fail to include in that history interpretation as it has been and is done by the Black man.

ADDITIONAL BLACK COURSES

Courses and/or seminars that could be added to the curriculum in the field of biblical studies might well include, for the sake of emphasizing the Black heritage, any that have to do with history, personalities, and cultural life. A seminar might deal with such a subject as, "The Black Man *in* the Bible." It would promote research on Black individuals and peoples as they appear in the biblical literature. The place of these individuals and peoples in Hebrew society could be noted, as could also the attitudes of the Hebrews to their presence. Another seminar might have to do with "The Black Man *and* the Bible." It would note how the Black man has been understood and treated upon the basis of biblical interpretation by White people and Black people through the years.

Apart from and in addition to such courses or seminars as I have suggested there are the following which appear in the curriculums of various seminaries under the heading of courses solely concerned with the Black church and/or community.

Black Bible and the Black Imagination
Black Hermeneutics and the Black Experience
The Person and Work of Jesus Christ
Cultural Background of the Old Testament
Gospel and World Issues

Church and Race in New Testament Times
Old Testament Book Studies
Nubian Language and Literature
Biblical Basis of Race Relations

All the enrichment possibilities and separate courses indicated thus far contribute to the enhancement of Black pride in the Black heritage and to the provision of information for Black people and White people with reference to the Black presence in the Bible. In addition to these, there are studies that might be organized in the biblical field which would permit analysis and investigation would be toward the end of noting liberating and survival values in that experience. On the one hand, the studies would inform Afro-Americans of those elements in their experience, past and present, and based upon the Bible, that have made for and continue to make for liberation and survival. On the other hand, they would inform others of values that might help to liberate them at points and enable them to live. It may be that the Black man, in his use of the Bible, has come closer to the reality that is God than some have ever dreamed.

That the Bible has played a vital role thus far in the life of Afro-Americans is attested on every hand. It is attested by the existence of the spirituals, which consist almost wholly of biblical themes and by the recollection and collection of sermons preached by Afro-Americans in days gone by—of which preachers James Weldon Johnson wrote that they were the mainspring of hope and inspiration of the Negro in America. Further, it is attested by the use of the Bible in gospel songs, jubilees, even purely secular songs. Indeed, much of the idiom and many of the thought forms of Afro-Americans are outright biblical.

That this was so from the beginning of the Black religious experience in America and continues to be so today constitutes one of the marvels of history. For even while the Bible was used (and is still used) to dehumanize him, the Black man found it to be the vehicle through which he experienced a liberating and sustaining God.

In the main, the seminars that would analyze and investigate the Black religious experience would be related to the fields of church history, theology, and practical studies. Titles which suggest themselves are:

The Bible in Black Religion and Theology
The Black Preacher and the Bible

The Bible and Oppressed Peoples
The Bible and Social Change
Use of the Bible in the Christian Education of
Oppressed Peoples
Biblical Religion and Native African Religions
Biblical Symbolism in Black Religion
The Bible in Black Liberation Movements

Thus far I have dealt with matters related to the one perspective. At the same time, however, I trust that I have answered some questions as well. Perhaps, despite what I have done, some will raise queries such as, "Does a teacher have to be Black in order to enrich present courses with the Black experience?" "Can only a Black teacher offer instruction in Black courses?" And the biggest question of all, "Should the Black experience be included in the curriculums of all Christian theological seminaries?" Of all the questions that anyone could ask—if the biblical content of the Black religious experience is that which has enabled the Afro-American to survive—then this last question is the most important of all. The question becomes not whether the Black experience should have a place only for Black students in Black theological schools but whether it can be excluded from the curriculum of any seminary in which students and all others would find their souls.

Chapter 2

The Black Man
in the Biblical World

During the course of centuries, upon the basis of the Bible the black man has been viewed in several and various ways. He has been regarded as the veritable father of Near Eastern civilizations; as cursed of God, or by a prophetic man of God, forever destined to serve "his more favored brethren," incapable of any civilization. At the same time, but still upon the basis of the Bible, he has been excluded from the family of man, and declared to be a beast. Moreover, he has been declared a non-inhabitant of the biblical world, yet at the same time the cause behind the disintegration and decay of ancient civilizations.

Upon the basis of non-biblical sources of knowledge he has been removed from the ancient biblical world, and excluded from those peoples which had a role in the development of civilization, modern as well as ancient.

The more or less biblically based view that regarded the black man as an inhabitant of the biblical world may be titled the "Old Hamite Hypothesis." Supported at points by the writings of ancients Greeks such as Homer and Herodotus, this hypothesis, like a stream, flowed in the area of Western thought for roughly four centuries, from 1400 to 1800. Then, around 1800, a new stream came to the surface. This latter, which may be called the "New Hamite Hypothesis,"[1] eliminates the black man, or rather the so-called Negro, from the biblical world. Those black

---

1. For a discussion of the New Hamite Hypothesis, see Edith R. Sanders, "The Hamite Hypothesis: Its Origin and Functions In Time Perspective," *Journal of African History*, x, 4(1969),pp.521-532.

peoples whom it retains are given the title Caucasoid Blacks who, instead of being regarded as Negroes, are viewed as being white.

Since 1800 the two streams have flowed side by side with the older becoming increasingly reduced in volume while the newer, especially in scholarly circles, has increased in size and significance to the extent that for many it is the only stream that exists. But more must be said about the streams in their concurrent flows. Each has been fed by numerous tributaries, sometimes by one and the same tributary. At times streamlets have flowed from one to the other, and so fed the waters that it is difficult, if not impossible, to distinguish them. Most especially is this true in regard to the Negro: the older stream fed by the tributary mistakenly called "the curse upon Ham" joins the waters of the newer that not only removes him from the biblical world but also views him as incapable of civilization.

Changing the figure of speech from streams to schools of thought, the two have given rise to interest, discussion, and debate. These have varied in intensity across the years since 1800, waxing and waning according to the social climate with respect to Negroes. Thus in the period leading up to the American Civil War, debate was at fever pitch. Again around the turn of the century interest, discussion and debate were renewed; and so still again after the United States Supreme Court's 1954 decision with respect to the segregation of Negroes.

Presently interest, if not discussion and debate, continues. With respect to biblical studies, on one side are critical historical-literary biblical scholars and their associates in the several related fields of science. They adhere to the newer school of thought; and the vast majority exclude the Negro from their writings, particularly as these have to do with the biblical world. Thus Heinisch-Heidt[2] in discussing the Table of Nations in Genesis 10 excludes Negroes along with several other peoples; and Martin Noth[3] allows a role for them "only on the border of the Near East as neighbors of Egypt...." Further, Noth criticizes the ancient Egyptians for having incorrectly portrayed and classified the Nubians as Negroes. Albright is a bit more generous in his inclusion of the Negro, writing as he does:

----

2. Dr. Paul Heinisch, *History of the Old Testament*, translated by William G. Heidt (St. Paul, Minnesota: The North Central Publishing Company, 1952), p.32.

3. *The Old Testament World*, translated by Victor I. Gruhn (Philadelphia: Fortress Press, 1969), p.236.

...All known ancient races in the region which concerns us here belonged to the so-called "white" or "Caucasian" race, with the exception of the Cushites ("Ethiopians") who were strongly Negroid in type, as we know from many Egyptian paintings.[4]

On the other side are those who still adhere to the older view upon the basis of their interpretation of the Bible, yet also upon the basis of evidence provided by archaeology, historical writings, and other sources. Some maintain that there was a very pronounced presence of blacks, even Negroes, in the biblical world, including the ancient Hebrews-Israelites-Jews.[5]

The present writer essays to investigate the validity of and to judge between the two opposing views. He does so, however, aware at the outset of several well nigh insoluble problems. In the main, these have to do with definitions and the usage of words, such as race, black, Negro, as they are employed by Afro-Americans on one hand and Euro-Americans on the other.

It is to be noted that Afro-Americans define black in several ways, both literal and figurative. Thus one may be literally black in color and be a black person, or Negro. Or the person may be of any shade of color and still be defined as Black, Negro. Additionally, one may be defined as black regardless of color or race; all who suffer oppression, especially oppression at the hands of white Westerners, are classified as black.

Over against the Afro-American definitions are the definitions of the white man. These may be social, political, biological, and so on. In America, black means Afro-American, Negro, but the precise definition may vary from state to state; or the definition may be set by the Federal Government. Nationally, anyone with a discernible trace of African Negro blood is a black.

Ethnologically, upon the basis of criteria established by white men, the color black may have nothing to do with race. A Negro is one who exhibits a certain group of traits which include

----

4. William Foxwell Albright, "The Old Testament World," *The Interpreter's Bible*, I, (New York-Nashville: Abingdon-Cokesbury Press, 1952), p.238.

5. In addition to works by Conservative and Traditionalist biblical scholars and other writers, there are numerous writings by Afro-Americans and Black Africans. Among these latter are *The Black Messiah* and *Black Christian Nationalism*, by Albert C. Cleague; and *From Babylon to Timbuktu*, by Rudolph R. Windsor.

black color, a particular type of hair, and skeletal structure, especially cranial.

In the essay, several categories of evidences are set forth. And toward the end of making the most accurate judgment, two types, of at times overlapping, evidence are employed. One type consists of evidence supplied by scholars who are adherents to the newer view; the other, of evidence employed by holders of the older view that the writer regards as tenable.

Upon the basis of available evidence, the biblical world is divided into three general regions as follows: Egypt-African Cush; Asiatic Cush; and Mediterranean Lands. The evidence is then presented according to categories under each respective region. For Egypt-African Cush the categories of evidence are: archaeological data; historical works; critical historical-literary biblical scholars; personal names and adjectives; modern travelers and anthropologists; ancient Greek and Roman writers; and early Christian commentators. The evidence for Asiatic Cush is subsumed under two categories: ancient Greek writers, and modern historical works. And for the Mediterranean Lands the evidence is presented under the one category of historical works. Finally, the evidences from the three regions are viewed from the vantage point of Hebrew-Israelite-Jewish accounts, traditions and legends: the biblical Table of Nations, the Babylonian Talmud, and Midrashim.

The present article is limited to a presentation of evidence for Egypt-African Cush, under the categories of archaeological data and historical works.

EGYPT-AFRICAN CUSH

Archaeological Data. The phrase archaeological data as here used applies to all those archaeological finds of antiquity that throw light on the subject and give content to the evidence. They may be observed and gathered from the surface or unearthed. Further, they may be of several kinds: written records of whatever description, paintings, statuary, skeletal remains.

With respect to Egypt-African Cush, antiquities have been better preserved than in any other place. Additionally the finds have been most numerous there; and the investigator might well begin in this region because of the sheer volume of evidence respecting the absence or presence of the black man. Moreover this region is part of the continent where in historical times the Blacks have constituted the bulk of the overall population. But there is still another reason for beginning with Egypt-African Cush. From the very beginning of modern Egyptology the black man, more particularly the Negro, has figured largely in the endeavor, albeit as an object rather than a participant. The New Hamite Hypothesis and Egyptology went and continue to go arm in arm. Up to roughly 1800 the ancient Egyptians as well as the ancient Cushites had been taken to be black and Negroes. Traditionally biblical interpretation, supported by observations of Herodotus, the so-called Father of History, served as the basis of the view. Illustrative of the Herodotus element are the words of Count Volney, after travels in Egypt and the Near East during the 1780's:

> I was at first tempted to attribute this [color of the Egyptians] to the climate (d) but when I visited the sphynx, I could not help thinking the figure of that monster furnished the true solution of the enigma: when I saw its features precisely those of a negro, I recollected the remarkable passage of Herodotus, in which he says, "For my part, I believe the Colchi to be a "colony of Egyptians," because, like them, they have black skins and frizzled hair (e):" that is, that the ancient Egyptians were real negroes, of the same species with all the natives of Africa...[6]

A few years after Count Volney's trip came Napoleon's invasion of Egypt, 1798, and the consequent opening up of Egypt for archaeological discovery. The New Hamite Hypothesis, from its beginning based upon theories about race which placed the Negro at the very bottom could not permit a possibility that Negroes had developed the civilization of the Nile Valley. And by 1810 Blumenbach, pioneer in racial classification, was in Egypt studying human remains. From those days until the present, Egyptology has continued with one underlying motive being to prove that the ancient Egyptians-African Cushites were not Negroes.

But modern Egyptology has been related to the Negro in still another way. It got under way at the very time that justifications for the enslavement of Negroes were feverishly being sought; and it became the handmaiden of both the Old Hamitic Hypothesis coupled with the curse upon Canaan (Ham),

----
6. M.C.F. Volney, *Travels Through Syria and Egypt*, translated from the French, Vol. I (London: G.G.J. and J. Robinson, 1787), pp. 80f.

and the New Hamite Hypothesis. It was in such an arrangement as this that the two streams flowed as one. In America there arose what has been called a "school of anthropologists" bent on debasing the Negro, and using Egyptology in such a way that one member of the school referred to his work as "niggerology."[7] And so on into the present, with Egyptologists either ignoring altogether a Negro presence or, at best, admitting of only a slight Negro element in the Cushite population. But now to a consideration of the archaeological evidence.

Recent archaeological discoveries establish in the Sahara a Negro civilization which goes back as far as 8000 B.C.[8] It is believed by some that with the increasing desiccation of the Sahara some of the inhabitants moved eastwards into the Nile Valley as well as southwards into so-called Negro Africa. But some New Hamite Hypothesis scholars concede that predynastic Egyptians were Negroid in whole or in part. Having made that concession, however, they progressively remove the Negro from the Egyptian population between the beginning of the dynastic period up to the Eighteenth Dynasty. Afterwards they admit of a presence to a very limited degree.

About a Negro presence across the centuries of the dynastic periods archaeology has much to say. After making allowance for explicit and implicit counter claims and for differences of opinion in regard to identification of lands and definitions of words, the following stand out.

Ancient Egyptian Historical Records. First there are among the archaeological data such records as were compiled by Breasted and Pritchard. Breasted's five volume work, *Ancient Records of Egypt*,[9] from beginning to end, is a documentary of references to Negroes, beginning with the Third Dynasty. From the period of the Third Dynasty there is the Palermo Stone with a

---

7. Samuel George Morton, George Robins Gliddon, Josiah Clark Nott, and others. For recent works on these men, see especially William Stanton, *The Leopard's Spots: Scientific Attitudes Toward Race In America* 1815-59 (Chicago and London: The Univerisity of Chicago Press, 1960).

8. See, for example, the following works: Henri Lhote, "The Fertile Sahara," *Vanished Civilizations of The Ancient World*, edited by Edward Bacon (New York-Toronto-London: McGraw-Hill Book Co., Inc., 1963) pp.11-32; Basil Davidson, *Africa: History of a Continent* (New York: The Macmillian Company, 1966); and James Wellard, *Lost Worlds of Africa* (New York: E.P. Dutton & Co., Inc., 1967).

9. James Henry Breasted, *Ancient Records of Egypt* (New York: Russell & Russell, Inc., 1906, reissued, 1962).

statement about "hacking up the land of the Negro." From the Sixth Dynasty, during the reign of Pepi I, there is the Inscription of Uni with its list of Bedwin Negro tribes against whom the Egyptians waged war; and from the reign of Mernere there are the Inscriptions of Harkhuf which include an account of a journey into the lands of the Negroes. The Twelfth Dynasty yields the "First Semneh Stela" with its prohibition against the crossing of a boundary at the second cataract of the Nile by any Negro except a tradesman or commissioned person. Between the Twelfth and Eighteenth Dynasties no inscriptions are presented, but from the Eighteenth Dynasty onwards they are numerous. In substance they have to do with references to Negro lands and peoples, with individual Negroes such as one or more who bear the name "Nehesi," with Negro captives of war and with Negroes in the armed forces on through inscriptions of the twenty-fifth Dynasty, the Ethiopian.

Pritchard's volume on *Ancient Near Eastern Texts*[10] supplements Breasted's volumes with an inscription attributed to Kamose who reigned just prior to the establishment of the Eighteenth Dynasty. A portion of the inscription is significant not only for what it adds to knowledge of Egyptian history but also for Pritchard's identification of Ethiopia (ancient Cush) with Negro. The relevant portion reads:

> ... [One] prince is in Avaris, another is in Ethiopia, and [here] I sit associated with an Asiatic and a Negro! Each man has his slice of this Egypt, dividing up the land with me....[11]

Beyond this contribution to the subject at hand, Pritchard's volume provides additional content by including a list of temple serfs from the reign of Ramses III, an Egyptian letter that deals with a mixed Egyptian military force of 5000 bowmen including 880 Negroes, and a letter from the Amarna period that bemoans the behavior of Cushite, Negro, troops in Canaan.

Additional inscriptions include that of Antef V, Eleventh Dynasty, which boasts of conquests over Asiatics and Negroes; that of Ameny, Twelfth Dynasty, which records campaigns

---

10. James B. Pritchard, *Ancient Near Eastern Texts Relating To The Old Testament*, Second Edition Corrected and Enlarged (Princeton, New Jersey: Princeton University Press, 1955).

11. Pritchard, p. 232. Attention should be given to Pritchard's footnote on the rendering Negro instead of Nubian.

against Ethiopians; and an inscription of Usertesen I, Twelfth Dynasty, reporting victory over several Negro tribes. And from the Thirteenth Dynasty comes a cartouche upon which is engraved the name Ra-Neshi, the Negro of Ra, identified as a king.[12]

Statuary and Paintings. Second among archaeological data are statuary and paintings of several kinds. Regarded by some as representing Negroes, they go back as early as 3000 B.C. and continue through dynastic and later times. Two limestone portraits which Reisner dated around 3000 B.C., and designated by him "the earliest known portraits of Negroes," were obtained by the Boston Museum.[13] From the Fourth Dynasty (2550 B.C.), comes the head of a princess whom William Stevenson Smith identifies as a member of the Cheops family. Writes Smith, "The wife of the other unknown Prince (G4440) is of negroid type with thick lips, wide nostrils, and full cheeks (Fig. 11) ...."[14] Montet refers to the head as being that of a Negro woman, and states that, being from Giza, it was probably made in the royal workshops for a member of the Cheop's family.[15]

And, commenting on the innumerable statues and statuettes that date from the period of the Old Kingdom, Montet writes that the men were on the whole rather tall, had broad, strong shoulders, a firm flat belly, and well developed limbs. "They had clearly defined features, prominent eyes, usually large, almost flat noses, thickish lips and somewhat low foreheads. Such were without exception the kings of Egypt at the time of the Old Kingdom."[16]

Other statuary indicative of a Negroid element in the general Egyptian population is that of individual rulers. Meriting

----

12. On these one may see William M. Flinders Petrie, A *History of Egypt*, Vol. I (Freeport, New York: Books For Libraries Press, 1902, reprinted 1972), pp. 137ff.

13. See Grace Hadley Beardsley, *The Negro in Greek and Roman Civilization* (New York: Russell & Russell, 1929, reissued 1967), p.12.

14. *Ancient Egypt*, Fourth Edition, Fully Revised (Boston: Beacon Press, 1961), p. 35.

15. Pierre Montet, *Eternal Egypt*, translated by Doreen Weightman (New York: The New American Library of World Literture, Inc., 1964), p. 27, and plate 29.

16. Ibid., p.25.

special mention, according to descriptions of some historians,[17] were Nefert-ari Ahmose, wife of Ahmose I, founder of the Eighteenth Dynasty, Thothmes I, Thothmes II, Seti I, Queen Tiy, wife of Amenophis III and Osorkon II. Taharqa of the Ethiopian Dynasty requires an additional word, for even most recent writers deem statues of him to be Negroid. There are those who see in the apparent Negro kneeling in submission to Esarhaddon on the Sinjirli stela none other than this pharaoh. And I. Woldering in discussing the art of the Ethiopian dynastic period writes, "King Taharka is shown with negroid features, which indicate the racial origin of the Nubian rulers."[18] And in discussing statuettes from the same period he goes on to say:

> In the case of female statuettes slender maidenly delicacy gives way to the stumpiness and corpulence typical of Nubian women. An ivory statuette of a lady of the royal family, now in Edinburgh, depicts her as thickset and plump. The face, with full lips and heavy eyelids, betrays her negroid racial origin.[19]

Painted limestone reliefs dating from the Middle Kingdom, Twelfth Dynasty (1991-1785), show Negroes of various ranks in society. Other well-known paintings depicting Negroes, by way of example, date from the reigns of Queen Hatshepsut, Tutankamun (Huy's tomb), Seti I, Ramses II and III. Some from the reigns of Seti I and Ramses II portray four races of men according to the Egyptians, in which are included the Egyptians themselves as reddish-brown and Negroes as black. The paintings in Huy's tomb are revelatory in regard to the

---

17. On the Negroid appearance of certain pharaohs, see: Sir J. Gardner Wilkinson, *The Manners And Customes Of The Ancient Egyptians*, New Edition Revised and Corrected by Samuel Birch, In Three Volumnes (Boston: S.E. Cassino and Company, 1883), Vol. I, p. 42 for Amenophis III; George Rawlinson, *A History of Ancient Egypt*, In Two Volumes, (New York: Dodd, Mead & Company, 1882), Vol. II, pp. 277 for Amenophis III and IV, p.294 for Ramses I, p. 440 for Osorkon II; George Rawlinson, *Ancient Egypt*, Third Edition (London: T. Fisher Unwin; New York: G.P. Putnam's Sons, 1887), pp. 158ff. for Thothmes I, pp. 204ff. for Thothmes II, pp. 250ff. for Seti I and Ramses II. For Nefert-ari-Ahmose, see the following: E.A. Wallis Budge, *The Dwellers On The Nile*, Fourth Edition (56, Paternoster Row: The Religious Tract Society, 18893), p. 69; Wilkinson, op. cit., Vol. I, p.37; and George Rawlinson, op.cit., Vol. II, pp. 215f.

18. Irmgard Woldering, *The Art of Egypt*, translated by Ann E. Keep (New York: Greystone Press, 1963), pp. 218f.

19. Ibid.

Negroid features of Nubians.   Describing one of them, Mariette-Bey wrote:

> ...People of every shade of complexion and of every race present themselves before him. Some are Negroes with distinctive features strongly marked; others are of the Negro type but brown in color...[20]

Skeletal Remains. Skeletal remains, especially skulls, have been studied and restudied in efforts to determine the percentage of Negroes in the population of Egypt across the centuries. During the first decades of the twentieth century, G. Elliot Smith, upon the basis of his anatomical studies, admitted of possibly 5% of Negroes in the predynastic period.[21]   More recently, upon the basis of a restudy of some crania and a study of some new ones, Eugen Strouhal allows of 1/3 Negroid and 1/3 Negroid-mixed for the population of one predynastic time.[22]   In 1905 Arthur Thompson and David Randall-MacIver in their book, *Ancient Races in the Thebaid* reported that of Egyptians belonging to the period between the Early Predynastic and Fifth Dynasty, 24% of the males and 19.5% of the females were to be classified as Negroes. Further, that for the periods of the Sixth to the Eighteenth Dynasty about 20% of the males and 15% of the females studied are grouped with Negroes.[23]   Prior to these, Auguste Mariette-Bey reported on skeletal remains at Thebes dating from the Eleventh Dynasty. Says he, "The inhabitants of Thebes interred at Drah-abou'l-neggah, the necropolis of that early period, were frequently Negroes."[24]

Modern Historical Works. To be sure, modern historians and other writers draw upon archaeology and related pursuits for the production of their works. Consequently, to use the finds of

----

20. Auguste Mariette-Bey, *The Monuments of Upper Egypt*, translated by Alphonse Mariette (London: Triibner & Co., 1877) pp. 225f. One should note later editions of this work for their reduction in references to Negroes.

21. G. Elliot Smith, *The Ancient Egyptians And Their Influence Upon The Civilization of Europe* (London & New York: Harper & Brothers, 1911), pp. 83f.

22. "Evidence Of The Early Penetration Of Negroes Into Prehistoric Egypt," *Journal of African History*, XII, I (1971), pp. 109.

23. For this report I am dependent upon W.E.B. Du Bois, *The World And Africa*, (New York: International Publishers, 1965), p. 107.

24. Mariette-Bey, op. cit. p. 147

archaeology and the works of historical writers as sister categories is to make for a great deal of repetition. Nevertheless it seems profitable to use the two categories despite the obvious duplication.

In addition to the observations of several historians on the Negroid appearance of various pharaohs and other noble persons is the historical content of their books relating to Blacks-Negroes. This content is of two kinds: general descriptions of the ancient Egyptians as a whole and treatments of affairs in which Negroes figure.

Several historians join the archaeologists in either recognizing the predynastic Egyptians as Negroid or as having been strongly mixed with Negroes.[25] Others essay to give a description of the overall appearance of the population. Such a description, in addition to that of Montet given above, is that of George Rawlinson:

> ...The fundamental character of the Egyptian in respect of physical type, language, and tone of thought, is Nigritic. The Egyptians were not negroes, but they bore a resemblance to the negro which is indisputable. Their type differs from the Caucasian in exactly those respects which when exaggerated produce the negro. They were darker, had thicker lips, lower foreheads, larger heads, more advancing jaws, a flatter foot, and a more attenuated frame....[26]

Various historians include Negroes in their detailing of Egyptian history from the Fourth Dynasty onward. During the Fourth-Sixth Dynasties the Egyptians had dealings with the Negroes of Central Africa and recruited Negro tribes into their armies, as is shown by Una's inscription. Budge,[27] Petrie,[28] and others[29] make use of this inscription and note that the Egyptians

---

25. Wilkinson-Birch, Vol. I, p. 2; Budge, *Egypt In The Neolithic And Archaic Periods* (Vol. I of *A History of Egypt*), Reprint after the Edition of 1902 (New York: Humanities Press, Inc., 1968),p.37, and others. See also Sir Alan Gardiner, *Egypt of The Pharaohs* (Oxford: The Clarendon Press, 1961), p.392.

26. *Ancient Egypt*, p.24.

27. Budge, op. cit., Vol. II, p. 101.

28. Petrie, op. cit., p.94.

levied tens of thousands of troops including Negroes from several tribes. Fairservis records that among the wives of the Theban King Mentuhotep II (Eleventh Dynasty) were several with Negro blood and some with body tatooing, indicative of the closeness of Africa to the southern Nomes.[30] The period of the Twelfth Dynasty is noted as one during which Egyptians had numerous relations with Cush; and several historians call special attention to the stela of Sesostris III at Semneh on which Negroes, with a few exceptions, are forbidden to cross the boundary. Dynasty Thirteen is marked as one during which a Negro king, Ra-Nehsi, ruled even in the Delta region,[31] and around the same time Kamose complains of being situated between the Asiatic and Negro kings, sharing rule with them.

The Eighteenth Dynasty is presented as one during which the Egyptians had increasingly numerous contacts with Negroes, and as one during which the rulers were largely of Negro extraction. To begin with, Nefertari, black queen of Ahmore I, is by some historians declared to be a "negress." The treasurer of Queen Hatshepsut is stated to be a Negro on the basis of his name, Nehsi. Thutmose I wars against Negroes, while Amenhotep III employs Negro auxiliaries in his armies. At the same time, in one instance during his reign, 740 Negroes are brought back as captives of war.[32] Negroes are seen as constituting part of the Egyptian army during the reign of Amenhotep IV, as indicated by the behavior of Negro troops in Canaan during the Tel-el-Amarna period. And during the same period Negroes are integrated into the life of the Underworld.[33] Additionally, Negroes are included in the historical works on the basis of the paintings in the tombs of Eighteenth Dynasty personalities.

References in the historical works to Negroes in Egyptian life during the Nineteenth Dynasty are numerous. Seti I's tomb

---

29. James Henry Breasted, *A History of Egypt*, Second Edition, Fully Revised (New York: Charles Scribner's Sons, 1924), p. 134.

30. Walter A. Fairservis, Jr., *The Ancient Kingdoms Of The Nile* (New York and Toronto: The New American Library, 1962), p. 101.

31. Good statements about Ra-Nehsi are made by Petrie, op. cit., pp. 202 and 221, and by Budge, Ibid., pp. 103f.

32. George Steindorff and Keith C. Seele, *When Egypt Ruled The East* (Chicago & London: The University of Chicago Press, 1957), p. 72.

33. Montet, op. cit., pp. 191f.

paintings as depicting Negroes among the four races are included by some; and attention is called to the large number of Negroes, especially in the armies, yet also elsewhere. In this regard Rawlinson states that whole tribes of Negroes were moved into Asia;[34] and Breasted notes that during the reign of Ramses II there were nearly 1000 Negro soldiers in a mixed army of some 5000.[35] Ramses III is represented as warring against Asiatics and Negroes; and as having among the slaves in the Temple estates approximately 5000 Syrians and Negroes.[36] Later, during the reign of Ramses XI, note is taken of a certain Pa-Nehsi who was Viceroy of Cush and Commander of the Army.[37]

During the periods between the Nineteenth and Twenty-fifth Dynasties, various historians make mention of Negroes in the army of Shishak, identify Osorkon I with Zerah the Ethiopian,[38] refer to Osorkon II as Negroid, and place a Nubian king in Thebes during the reign of Osorkon III.[39]

To end with the Twenty-fifth Dynasty, Albright and Steindorff-Seele admit of a strong mixture of Negro blood in the veins of the Nubians-Ethiopians-Cushites; and it is generally admitted that Taharqa and his successors were of Negro extraction. Steindorff-Seele even go so far as to call special attention that under Taharqa "the throne of Egypt was occupied by a Negro king from Ethiopia!"[40] Arthur Weigall goes still further in his treatment of Piankhi, predecessor of Taharqa: he refers to him as the most famous of the "nigger kings."[41]

----

34. Rawlinson, op. cit., Vol. II, p. 323.

35. Op. cit., p.449.

36. John A. Wilson, *The Culture of Ancient Egypt* (*Chicago* and London: The University of Chicago Press, 1951), p.257.

37. *Ibid.*, p. 282.

38. E.A.W. Budge, *A History Of The Egyptian People*, New Edition (New York: E.P. Dutton & Co., 1923), p. 128.

39. Ibid., p. 130.

40. Op. cit., p. 271.

41. *Personalities of Antiquity* (New York: The H.W. Wilson Company, 1932), p. 186.

Chapter 3

Blacks and Jews in Historical Interaction: The Biblical/African Experience

The subject before us for consideration is part of a larger one, in the light of which it must be studied and only in the light of which it can be understood. That larger subject is: "Blacks and Jews in Historical Interaction: The Biblical/Black Experience." But having stated the larger subject of which the immediate one is only a part takes us short distance in dealing with it. Before real treatment can be given it is necessary first of all to establish a foundation upon which a superstructure can be erected. The foundation consists in confirming the existence of Black peoples in the Biblical world with whom Jews could have interacted; it cannot be taken for granted that there were. Once such a confirmation is made, then and then only, may the presentation proceed. For this reason the paper consists of two parts, the foundation and the superstructure.

The existence of black peoples in the Biblical world, especially of so-called Negroes, with whom ancient Jews could have interacted, is a matter of great interest, discussion, debate, and of confusing, contradictory opinions. Within modern times, in Western civilization, two diametrically opposed views have developed, with several sub-views between two extreme positions. From the introduction of Blacks, especially those who came to be called Negroes, into the consciousness of Western

Europeans around 1450 C.E. until roughly 1800 C.E. there was one view rather commonly held in both the popular and scholarly mind. This view was that the Hamites referred to in the Bible were peoples black in color, and generally regarded as what were called Negroes. It may be called the old, traditional Hamite view; and was based upon the Genesis account of Noah's sons,[1] particularly Ham-Canaan, and upon the so-called Table of Nations in Genesis 10 and I Chronicles 1, which lists Ham and his descendants. At times the view was associated with Noah's curse of Canaan, interpreted more frequently to be a curse of Ham and his descendants, at times not, on the basis of which curse the Hamites were destined to be slaves of the families of Shem and Japheth, and to be black in color—despite the fact that in the Biblical accounts Ham is not cursed, nor is color mentioned or even implied unless of course the word Ham in Hebrew meant black at the times the stories and the Table originated.

Additionally, although a rival view came into existence around 1800 C.E., this traditional Hamite view continued to be held; and associating Hamites with Blacks/Negroes especially, and further associating these people with Noah's curse of (Ham)-Canaan, it was employed to justify the enslavement of black Africans. This use was made to the fullest between the year 1800 and the American Civil War. But the emancipation of Blacks from slavery did not terminate the usage. The practice has continued in America and elsewhere, at times receiving greater emphasis than at others, as in the United States of America during the years immediately after the 1954 Supreme Court decision in regard to segregation in education. Some traditionalist, conservative "Christians" resurrected the view and employed it as a divine justification for the continued segregation of Blacks. Twenty years later the view is still adhered to by many.

Dissociated from the curse of (Ham)-Canaan, and/or in spite of the association, the traditional Hamite view was and still is used in favor of black peoples including the so-called Negroes.[2] According to this usage, which has been made by some Whites and by numerous black individuals and groups, the Biblical Hamites were Negroes and included the Hamites listed in

----
1. Genesis 9.

2. See the book *Yaradee: A Plea for Africa*, by Frederick Freeman (Philadelphia, 1836), and also histories of the Afro-Americans written by Black authors from 1840 to the present.

the Biblical Table of Nations, notably: Egyptians, African Cushites (Ethiopians), and Asiatic Cushites of South Asia, Mesopotamia, Phoenicia, and Canaan. These peoples, taken to be black in color, are regarded as the founders of the great ancient civilizations of the Middle East. And, to be sure, according to the Biblical accounts, Jews were in interaction with all of them.

Over against the traditional view, whether or not associated with the curse of (Ham)-Canaan, there came into being around 1800, as has been stated, a new Hamite hypothesis or view.[3] It dissociates the so-called Negroes from the Hamites, removes color from the criteria for determining racial identity, and regards black non-Negroids to be white—Caucasoid or Europid Blacks. It is this view or hypothesis which came to characterize the so-called sciences of anthropology, ethnology, and kindred studies, but also critical historical-literary Biblical studies. And just as anthropology and ethnology removed Negroes from the Biblical world so did critical study of the Bible remove Negroes from the Bible and Biblical history—except for an occasional Negro individual who could only have been a slave. Thus today in critical Biblical studies, as in anthropology and ethnology, the ancient Egyptians, Cushites, in fact all the Biblical Hamites, were white; so-called Negroes did not figure at all in Biblical history, and there could not have been interaction between Blacks and Jews if by Blacks is meant so-called Negroes.

He who would build the superstructure called for by the title of this paper is thus faced with the further task of choosing between Scylla and Charybdis, between two diametrically opposed views: one that allows for an interaction, one that does not.

In an endeavor to find the truth of the matter the writer undertook research which now permits of rather well supported conclusions.[4] Making use of what he regarded to be tenable supports for the traditional Hamite views, and supports supplied by adherents to the newer view, including critical Biblical scholars, he assembled several categories of evidence that testify to a Black, including Negro, presence in the Biblical world. This

----

3. For a discussion of the new Hamite hypothesis, see Edith R. Sanders, "The Hamite Hypothesis," *Journal of African History*, X (1969), pp. 521-532.

4. See the essay by the writer entitled "The Black Man in the Biblical World," published in the Spring issue 1974 of *The Journal of the Interdenominational Theological Center*.

Black presence was to be found in Egypt, African Cush, Asiatic Cush, and in eastern Mediterranean lands.

For Egypt-African Cush the categories of evidence are: archaeological data, consisting of Egyptian-Cushite written records, paintings, sculptures, and skeletal remains; modern historical works; critical Biblical scholarly works; personal names and adjectives; opinions of modern travelers, archaeologists and anthropologists; ancient Greek-Roman legends and historical writings; works of early Christian commentators; and ancient Jewish writings, including the Bible, Babylonian Talmud, Midrashim, and legends. Categories of evidence for Asiatic Cush are: writings of ancient Greeks; modern historical works; archaeological data; and ancient Jewish works, the same as above. And for the Mediterranean lands, archaeological data and modern historical works are the categories.

The evidences testify that, according to American sociological definitions of Negro, the ancient Egyptians were Negroes; that according to modern anthropological and ethnological definitions the ancient Egyptian population included a large percentage of so-called Negroes, possibly 25% as an average across the long period of time that was ancient Egyptian history. They indicate that the African Cushites (Ethiopians) were predominantly of Negroid identity; and that Blacks, including Negroes, during Biblical times, inhabited parts of Asia from the Indus River Valley westwards into Elam-Persia, Mesopotamia, parts of Arabia, Phoenicia, Canaan, Crete, and Greece. Further, the evidences indicate that, *in the main*, wherever in the Bible Hamites are referred to they were people who, today in the Western world, would be classified as Black, and Negroid. Additionally, they establish a Black element within the ancient Hebrew-Israelite Jewish population itself.

With respect to the superstructure that may now be erected, it may be done in several ways. This essay proceeds by pointing to interactions across the years of Biblical history in chronological sequence, beginning with the prehistoric period. Materials used will be mainly conditions and events of history as these are set forth in the Bible, supplemented by archaeology, and "Legends of the Jews."

First of all, it is to be noted that in prehistoric times, before the coming of the Hebrews to Canaan, and also during the time of Hebrew-Israelite-Jewish occupation, Negroid peoples lived in the land, apart from any black element in the Hebrew-Israelite-Jewish population.[5] Shortly after 2000 B.C.E., a time when even new Hamite hypothesis advocates claim the so-called Negro first appeared in history, the Patriarchal period began. At the beginning of this period, according to one Biblical tradition, the patriarch Abraham migrated from what later came to be called Chaldea, a land occupied by Cushites. Jewish legend has it that Abraham and his people suffered persecution at the hands of none other than Nimrod, the Cushite founder of Mesopotamian civilization and culture.[6] According to another tradition, which is not necessarily in conflict with the other, Abraham's starting place was Haran in northwestern Mesopotamia. From this region he migrated into Canaan where he moved among Hamites and non-Hamites, remaining aloof from all, and refusing to permit intermarriage. From predominantly Hamite Canaan he moved to Egypt where despite the designs of a Hamite pharaoh upon Sarah the tribal blood remained pure. Nevertheless the patriarch himself produced a son by an Egyptian woman who herself later on obtained an Egyptian wife for the son. Under Isaac and Jacob, according to the prevailing tradition, there was no regular intermarriage with the Hamitic Canaanites. But in Canaan Esau and Judah engaged in marriage with Canaanite women;[7] and, whatever were the Hebrew tribes that migrated to and settled in Egypt during the patriarchal age, in that land occurred a significant infusion of black blood. Joseph married an Egyptian wife to whom were born two of the more important Hebrew tribes, Ephraim and Manasseh. Apart from and in addition to the interactions occasioned by such a marriage as that of Joseph, there were interactions arising from the Hebrew state of affairs during the period of Egyptian sojourn. Whether or not the Hebrew settlement was related to the Hyksos invasion and occupation of Egypt, the first years saw a favorable position. The latter years saw a state of oppression, with concomitant reactions, and it was these that the Jews best remembered. But more remains to be said about the infusion of black blood into the Hebrew tribe or tribes in Egypt, through Moses and his family, with all the implications for Black/Negro-Jewish interactions. The book of Exodus records Moses' escape from Egypt to Midian where the daughters

----

5. See Anati, Emmanuel, *Palestine Before the Hebrews*, page 322; and McCown, Chester C., *The Ladder of Progress in Palestine*, pages 130, 142 f., 166.

6. See, for example, *The Talmud*, by H. Polano, pages 30 ff. for one such story.

7. Genesis 36, 38.

of Jethro, on the basis of his appearance, mistakenly identified him to be an Egyptian, and where Moses married Zipporah, one of Jethro's daughters. Then the book of Numbers states that Moses had married a Cushite woman who very well could have been none other than a Cushite Zipporah herself, Cushites having been inhabitants of Arabia and adjacent regions as well as Africa. Josephus, and Jewish spinners of legends were later to say much about Moses' marriage to a Cushite woman in spite of some rabbinic explanations to the contrary.[8] Furthermore, there are good grounds for believing that the tribal family of Moses was of black Cushite origin. Support for the opinion comes in the form of Egyptian names carried by members of the family as well as by other Hebrews: Moses, Phinehas, Hophni, Merari, Pashur, etc., especially Phinehas, which means Black, Negro, Nubian, etc.[9] This last name, it is to be observed, was the name of a grandson of Aaron, and was carried by members of the priesthood through the period of the Babylonian exile.

Still further, indications of interactions between Black Africans and possibly Hebrew tribes in Canaan during the patriarchal period lie in the Tel-el-Amarna correspondence. According to one communication Black/Negro troops in the Egyptian army were plundering the community because they had not received their pay.[10]

During the period of the conquest and settlement of Canaan, the period of the judges, interactions between Hamites-Jews are to be seen in the several Biblical accounts that have to do with relations between Hebrews and Canaanites and between Hebrews and Cushites. In these accounts there are directives against intermarriage, and the beginnings of amalgamation of the Canaanites. There is also the recounting of an invasion and oppression by a Mesopotamian ruler with the name Cushanrishathaim—the "Cushite of double infamy." And toward the end of the period pristine Hebrew religion was Canaanized-Africanized, and thus polluted, by fertility practices instituted by Eli's Egyptian-Cushite named priest-sons, Phinehas and Hophni.[11]

----

8. Josephus, Flavius, *Antiquities of the Jews*, Book II, Chapter 10, translated by William Whiston. For a contrary view see Ginzberg L., *Legends of the Jews*, VI, 90, as referred by Henry S. Noerdlinger, *Moses and Egypt*, page 70.

9. Albright, W.F., *From the Stone Age to Christianity*, pages 193 f.; *Yahweh and the Gods of Canaan*, page 165.

10. Pritchard, James B., *Ancient Near Eastern Texts Relating to the Old Testament*, page 232.

11. I Samuel 2.

For the period of the United Monarchy interactions are to be noted in the accounts of relations between the Israelites-Judeans and Canaanites and Phoenicians; in the account of the Cushite messenger in David's army;[12] in the accounts of Solomon's dealings with the king of Egypt and marriage to an Egyptian princess; in the narrative about the Queen of Sheba; and in the accounts of Hadad's and Jeroboam's flight to protection under the king of Egypt.

References to interactions during the two hundred-year history of the two kingdoms are in the several narratives of Jeroboam's return from Egypt, Shishak's invasion of Judah-Israel, and the invasion of Zerah, the Cushite. Additionally, they appear in the narratives and oracles of the 8th century B.C.E. recorded in Kings-Chronicles and in the books of Amos and Hosea. Within the prophetic books are Amos' comparison of Yahweh's equal regard for Israelites and Cushites (Ethiopians, Negroes);[13] and Hosea's castigation of Israel for her wishy-washy trust in Assyria and Egypt instead of trust in Yahweh. Possibly also interactions are to be seen in the account of the repopulation of Israel with outsiders by the Assyrians.[14]

For the remainder of the 8th century, that is, from 721 B.C.E. to the end of the century, interactions between Blacks and Judeans may be viewed in clearest light. This period was that of the early years of the 25th Egyptian Dynasty, the Cushite or Ethiopian. In the Bible itself the view is provided by the book of Isaiah son of Amoz, with its several references to the Egyptians-Cushites.[15] In content the references range from complimentary descriptions of Cushites to warnings against trust in Egyptian-Cushite military strength, and prophecies that the Assyrians will make of the Egyptians-Cushites captives of war. Also indicative of Black-Judean interactions is the narrative of Chaldean intrigue in Judah toward the end of the century by Merodach-baladan; and the other anti-foreigner oracles in the book. Additionally, during the period 727-700 B.C.E. both Israel and Judah were allies of Egypt-Cush.

Interactions between Blacks and Judeans during the period 700-582-570 B.C.E. were both internal within the Judean

----
12. II Samuel 18.

13. 9:7.

14. II Kings 17:24ff.

15. Chapters 18, 19, 20, 30, and 31.

community, and external in the books of II Kings and II Chronicles, and in the prophetic books of Zephaniah, Jeremiah, and Ezekiel. Zephaniah himself is said to have been the son of one Cushi,[16] and his family tree is traced back to a certain Hezekiah whom some Biblical scholars identify with Hezekiah, the Judean king.[17] Assuming, as do several Biblical scholars of note, that Zephaniah was a black Judean,[18] and that his ancestry included King Hezekiah, Blacks were among the population, and black blood flowed in the veins of Judah's kings.

The book of Jeremiah makes mention of a Jehudi, great grandson of one Cushi, who was sent by the princes of Judah to Baruch, Jeremiah's scribe, and who read Jeremiah's oracles dictated to Baruch, Jeremiah's scribe, and who read Jeremiah's oracles dictated to Baruch in the hearing of King Jehoiakim.[19] Additionally it contains an adage with respect to the Cushite's color as being unchangeable; narratives concerning a Cushite friend and helper of Jeremiah, Ebed-Melech; oracles against foreign nations including Egypt and other Hamites; and narratives about the fall of Judah to the Chaldeans and about Judean communities in exile in various parts of Egypt. It may be noted that the references to Blacks in the book of Jeremiah indicate that there was a Black element in the Judean population; that black Cushites were sufficiently well known that they could furnish an analogy between unchangeable color and behavior; and that members of the court included black Cushites. Further, and interesting to note incidentally, is the name of one of the places where Judean exiles settled in Egypt—Tahpanhes, "Fort of the Negro."

The book of Ezekiel, as does the book of Jeremiah, contains oracles against Hamites, including Phoenicians, Egyptians, and Cushites. Like the book of Jeremiah also, it permits a view of Judah in exile, in Chaldea, where the Judeans lived under rather favorable circumstances. At the same time it

---

16. Zephaniah 1:1.

17. A survey of Biblical *Introductions* reveals the following: E. Sellin wrote in 1923 that Zephaniah is generally held to have been a prophet of royal blood; among those who support the view are J.A. Bewer, R.K. Harrison, E.A. Leslie, R.H. Pfeiffer, and Charles L. Taylor, Jr.

18. Some who identify the prophet as a "Negro" are: Aage Bentzen, J.A. Bewer, Curt Kuhl, E. Sellin and A. Weiser. but note the contrary view of Georg Fohrer in his revision of Sellin's *Introduction*.

19. Chapter 36:14ff.

asserts that Judah's origins were mixed, and criticizes Judah for her whoredoms with the Assyrians, Chaldeans, and Egyptians.

And the historical books of Kings-Chronicles narrate the fall of Judah, the capture of Jerusalem, the destruction of the Temple—the most tragic experience for Judeans-Jews in Old Testament history, at the hands of the Chaldeans. These events made for the most hostile interactions between the Judeans-Jews and a people regarded as black—not only at that time, but for times to come, whenever they were remembered. In the meantime, between 609-586 B.C.E., Egypt was alternately an antagonist-protagonist with respect to Judah.

With the entrance of the Persians into Judean-Jewish life in 538 B.C.E., a new era of interactions began. In the Persian-Elamite population, and in the Persian army were Blacks.[20] Relations between the two peoples were good; so good in fact that someone has remarked that only in the instance of the ancient Persians did the ancient Jews have only good to say. But the Bible, supplemented by extra-Biblical materials such as the Elephantine papyri and Jewish Midrashim and legends, provides still more insights into Black-Jewish interactions during the Persian period which for Jews may be said to have lasted from 540 B.C.E. until the beginning of the Greek Period under Alexander the Great in 332 B.C.E. There are the hopes and aspirations for a going forth from Babylon back to Palestine, and the general universalism voiced by a Second Isaiah; there are the lofty universalistic passages of a Trito-Isaiah that envision a time when Assyria and Egypt will be accepted on par with Israel by Yahweh, and when Yahweh's temple shall be a house of prayer for all peoples. At the same time there are passages such as the anti-Chaldean Psalm 137, and the Trito-Isaianic passages that envision the day when Blacks and others shall serve Israel.[21] There are also the interactions revealed by the Elephantine papyri with their record of a Jewish community in Upper Egypt that has suffered at the hands of native Egyptians. Perhaps most significantly of all, there are the anti-Black traditions and legends that began to come into existence at least by the time of Ezra, around 400 B.C.E., many of which were recorded in the Babylonian Talmud and in the Midrashim. These are the "Ham"

----

20. See, for example Childe, V.G., *The Most Ancient East*, page 144; Olmstead, A.T., *History of the Persian Empire*, pages 238 ff.; M. Dieulafoy, *The Acropolis of Susa* (English Title); J.A. de Gobineau; and the ancient histories of G. Maspero, and George Rawlinson.

21. Isaiah 60,61.

stories, and legends about the origin of black Jews whether in Palestine or in Africa. And here it is to be noted that the stock of "Ham" stories continued to grow, after the Biblical period, on beyond the time when a historical gap between East and West was created by Islamic hegemony over the Near and Middle East, and westward over parts of the Mediterranean world.[22]

Not to be excluded for insights into Black-Jewish relations during the Persian period are the numerous particularistic and universalistic passages in the prophetic books of Joel, II Zechariah, chapters 9-14 of the book, and Malachi. Generally speaking, Jewish attitudes in these books include extremes of both particularism and universalism.

Between the end of the Persian period and the writing of the latest books in the Bible, interactions between Blacks and Jews are to be seen in the books of Maccabees wherein Jewish history during the Greek period is recounted; in the Gospel according to Matthew, with its narrative of the "Flight into Egypt"; in the book of Acts with its accounts of Jews present from all the world in Jerusalem on the Day of Pentecost, of Niger among the followers of Jesus at Antioch in Syria, and of Philip's conversion of the Ethiopian eunuch; and in the writings of Josephus. The books of Maccabees show Jewish relations with Egypt. Matthew depicts Egypt as still a haven for Jews persecuted in the homeland, yet tying residence in Palestine with coming out of Egypt. The book of Acts lists adherents to Judaism from countries inhabited by Blacks, and indicates that black people were among the early members of the Christian Church. And Josephus, who recounts the history of his people, including much about Moses and Cushites, goes into lengthy dissertations about the provenance of the Jews and their affinities with the Egyptians.[23]

Reviewing and summarizing, there were Black-Jewish interactions during the entire course of Biblical history. These interactions may be seen in the Bible, supplemented by archaeological data, the works of Josephus, and by extra-Biblical Jewish traditions, Biblical interpretations such as appear in the Babylonian Talmud and Midrashim, and legends. In the main,

---

22. On the dates for the Talmud and Midrashim, one may consult I. Epstein (in *The Interpreter's Dictionary of the Bible*), who gives a brief bibliography. An excellent discussion is presented in *White Over Black* by Winthrop D. Jordan; and there are numerous collections of interpretations and legends in L. Ginzberg's *Legends of the Jews*, and in books by S. Baring-Gould, H. Polano, and Samuel Rapaport.

23. *Against Apion* (Whiston's translation).

except for the relatively few universalist passages in the Bible, the reactions, which are from the Jewish side only, are negative in nature,   And in the Babylonian Talmud, Midrashim, and legends the reactions are wholly anti-Black, despite the conclusion that Blacks formed a part of the ancient Hebrew-Israelite-Jewish community.

Chapter 4

Egypt and Ethiopia
in the Old Testament

In the King James and Revised Standard Versions of the Bible, the word "Egypt" (Mitzraim in Hebrew) along with cognates, occurs some seven hundred forty times in the Old Testament.[1] The word translated Ethiopia and/or Cush (Cush in Hebrew) along with cognates, and including three instances of duplication in the references, appears fifty-eight times in the King James Version. In this version the translation "Ethiopia" is used thirty-nine times; "Cush" (untranslated) with cognates, nineteen times. The numerous references to Egypt led one Old Testament scholar to remark, "No other land is mentioned so frequently as Egypt in the Old Testament....To understand Israel one must look well to Egypt."[2]

The occurrences of the words are in several types of the Old Testament literature including the Pentateuch, or five books of the Law, the historical books, the books of prophecy, and in the poetical-wisdom books, but not in all the thirty-nine books that constitute the Protestant Old Testament. Additionally, the literature in which the references occur dates from all periods in the literary history from the time of the Hebrew patriarchs (ca. 1800 B.C.E.) down to and including the Hellenistic period in Biblical history (332-141 B.C.).

In this essay the main references to Egypt are classified and presented under seven headings as follows:

---

1. This number makes allowance for duplication.

2. John Paterson, "The Old Testament World," in *The Bible and History*, ed. by William Barclay (Nashville and New York: Abingdon Press, 1968), p.39.

1. As the name of a person.
2. In narratives of the Hebrew patriarchs and Joseph
3. In narratives of the enslavement, Moses, and the exodus.
4. With reference to the Hebrews having been brought out of Egypt.
5. In prophetic oracles.
6. Egypt in historical relations with Israel-Judahites-Jews.
7. In poetical-wisdom literature.

References to Ethiopia/Cush are arranged and discussed under the following five captions:

1. As a term of identification.
2. As a geographical reference.
3. In prophetic oracles.
4. Ethiopia/Cush in historical relations with Judahites.
5. In poetical-wisdom literature.

EGYPT

Egypt (Mitzraim) as the Name of a Person

Four times Egypt appears in the Old Testament as the name of a person (Genesis 10:6, 13f, duplicated in I Chronicles 1:8, 11). In these instances Egypt is stated to be the (eponymous) ancestor of the Egyptian people and of peoples descended from them. Important to note among the descendants are the Philistines, a fact that may well point to Egyptian relations with the island of Crete.[3]

In Narratives of the Hebrew Patriarchs and Joseph

Beginning in Genesis, chapter 12:10 and continuing through the end of the book, there are seventy-nine occurrences of the word Egypt. These are contained in the accounts of the three Hebrew patriarchs, Abraham, Isaac, and Jacob, and of Joseph. Recounted are Abraham's going down to Egypt with his entourage during a time of famine in his adopted home, the land of Canaan; and the bestowal of riches upon Abraham by the

---

3. See, for example, R.K. Harrison, *Old Testament Times* (Grand Rapids, Michigan: William B. Eerdmans Publishing Company, 1970), pp. 171ff.

Pharaoh who had taken Abraham's professed sister, but really his wife, into his harem, and the Pharaoh's expulsion of Abraham upon his learning through plagues that Sarah was Abraham's wife and before he had intercourse with her. It is recounted further that Abraham had an Egyptian maid, Hagar, by whom he sired his first-born son, Ishmael, for whom Hagar obtained an Egyptian wife (Genesis 16:1, 3; 21:9). Isaac is said to have been instructed not to go down to Egypt (Genesis 26:2).

The references with regard to Jacob are interwoven with the accounts concerning Joseph. They relate that during a time of famine in Canaan, Jacob learned that food was available in Egypt where his favorite son, Joseph, had been sold some years previously. After reestablishing relations with Joseph, Jacob moved with his entire family to Egypt. There he died, but he was buried in Canaan, mourned by Egyptians as well as by Hebrews (Genesis 50:3-13).

The narratives that recount the story of Joseph contain the largest number of references to Egypt in the book of Genesis. In what is really a series of stories there is narrated Joseph's being sold as a slave in Egypt to an Egyptian officer whose wife attempted to seduce him; his refusal to cohabit with the woman on moral and religious grounds, and consequent imprisonment on the false charge of attempted rape; and his interpretation of the Pharaoh's troublesome dreams through a God-given ability in consequence of which the Pharaoh elevated him to a position second only to his own. Further, the Pharaoh gave him an Egyptian wife, Asenath, by whom he had two sons, Manasseh and Ephraim. As the Pharaoh's vice-regent, so the stories continue, Joseph was placed over the fiscal affairs of Egypt in which position he enabled the country to survive seven years of famine which followed seven years of plenty, with sufficient food for export. Moreover, Joseph obtained the whole of the land of Egypt for the Pharaoh's personal possession. Upon his death Joseph was embalmed but not buried in Egypt. His body was kept unburied in anticipation of the Hebrew's return to Canaan where his burial place was to be.

A question arises: to what extent are the narratives of the patriarchs and Joseph records of actual historical events? In reply John Bright in his book, *A History of Israel*, writes that neither upon the basis of the Biblical chronology nor upon the basis of extra-biblical evidence can one place the patriarchs (and Joseph) within any particular century or centuries. Neither can they be identified as individual personalities. Continuing, he states that it is impossible to relate any person or event in Genesis 12-50 to any person or event otherwise known (in Egyptian history) and thereby establish a synchronism.[4] Similar statements are made by other scholars such as Henry Thomas Frank who in his book, *Bible, Archaeology, and Faith*, states "We have no direct reference outside the Bible to any Biblical figure before the monarchy"—that is, before 1000 B.C.[5] Additionally, the Biblical accounts do not provide the missing links which would enable us to place the kings and their people (here with reference to Egypt and Ethiopia) in a precise historical framework.[6]

Despite such statements as the foregoing, Biblical historians, on the basis of the Biblical narratives and archaeology, do arrive at definite and positive answers—one liberal, the other conservative. Seeing at least some historical value in the Biblical accounts, the liberals view Abraham, Isaac, and Jacob as heads of tribal movements rather than as father, son, and grandson who succeeded each other as the head of a single family group. Many associate the sale of Joseph into Egypt with the Hyksos period (ca. 1720-1550 B.C.).[7]

On the other hand, taking the Biblical narratives as actual historical accounts, the historical accuracy of which is guaranteed by the Bible's being literally the Word of God, conservative scholars are able to give exact dates for the patriarchs and Joseph as individual persons, and to relate them to specific persons and events in Egyptian history. Thus, conservatives are able to say dogmatically that Abraham was in Egypt between 2091 and 1991 B.C.; that Jacob went with his family to Egypt around 1876 B.C.; and that the Pharaoh who "knew not Joseph" was a Hyksos ruler rather than one of the 18th or 19th dynasties.

Specifically, Merrill F. Unger in his book, *Archaeology and The Old Testament*, is able to state categorically that the patriarchs were in Palestine contemporaneously with the Middle Kingdom in Egypt under the Twelfth dynasty (2000-1780 B.C.). He associates Jacob and Joseph with some Pharaoh of this dynasty, Amenemes I-IV or Senworset I-III and places the Hebrews in Egypt during the Hyksos period (1780-1546 B.C.).

---

4. Op. cit, (3rd ed. Philadelphia: Westminster Press, 1981), p.83.

5. Op. cit, (Nashville-New York: Abingdon Press, 1971), p.64.

6. Op. cit. (New York: Alfred A. Knopf, 1963), p.377.

7. For such views, see, for example, John Bright, op.cit. p. 87; H. Jagersma, *A History of Israel in the Old Testament Period*, translated by John Bowden from the Dutch (Philadelphia: Fortress Press, 1979), p. 46; and Theodore H. Robinson, *A History of Israel*, Vol. I (Oxford: Clarendon Press, 1932), p.63.

He places their enslavement in Egypt during the reign of Thutmose III of the 18th dynasty (1482-1450 B.C.).[8]

Leon Wood goes further and names the pharaoh whose dream Joseph interpreted as Senusert II (1994-1878 B.C.), and has Joseph dying during the reign of Amenemhet II (1841-1797 B.C.), approximately twenty-five years prior to the end of the Twelfth dynasty.[9] In very substantial agreement with Unger and Wood is Charles F. Aling in his book, *Egypt and Bible History*.[10]

In Narratives of the Enslavement, Moses, and the Exodus

Eighty-one times Egypt is referred to in the accounts of the enslavement of Hebrews in Egypt, of Moses, and of the Exodus from Egypt. In these accounts, as may be observed in those concerning the patriarchs and Joseph, Egypt is referred to most often as the *locus* of events.

Following a recounting of the enslavement of the Hebrews for security reasons subsequent to Joseph's death by a Pharaoh who knew nothing of Joseph there is given an account of the birth of Moses into a Hebrew family and his adoption by a daughter of Pharaoh. This is followed by a second account which tells of the murder of an Egyptian taskmaster, and Moses' consequent flight from Egypt to Midian. In this latter land, as the account continues, Moses was identified as an Egyptian, married and sired two sons, remained for forty years during which time he worked for his father-in-law as a shepherd, and received a call from the God of the Hebrew fathers under a hither-to unknown name, Yahweh, to return to Egypt in order to free the Hebrew slaves. In turn, Moses returned to Egypt where with his brother Aaron, he labored to obtain release of the Hebrews. During this time, God sent a series of plagues which affected the Egyptians but not the Hebrews in order to induce the Pharaoh to free the Hebrews. Through a final plague, the death of the first-born of all the Egyptians, God forced the Pharaoh to give in. Upon second thought, the Pharaoh sent his army in pursuit only to have

---

8. Op. cit. (Grand Rapids, Michigan: Zondervan Publishing House, 1954), p. 107ff.

9. Leon Wood, *A Survey of Israel's History* (Grand Rapids, Michigan: Zondervan Publishing House, 1970), p. 33ff.

10. Op. cit. (Grand Rapids, Michigan: Baker Book House, 1981).

it drowned in the waters of a sea through which the Hebrews passed on dry land.

With respect to the enslavement of Hebrews in Egypt, Moses, and the Exodus and their relationships to actual history, we have the same situation as that concerning the patriarchs and Joseph.

Liberal scholars are able to see an enslavement of a few Hebrews, perhaps under Ramses II (1290-1224), Moses as an actual person who fought for the liberation of his people, and an exodus of a few thousand at most during the reign of Ramses II or of his son, Merneptah (1224-1214 B.C.)[11]

On the other hand, conservative scholar Leon Wood[12] states that the Pharaoh who "knew not Joseph" and places the Hebrews in bondage was the first Hyksos ruler, around 1730 B.C., seventy-five years after Joseph's death. Moses was born in 1526, during the reign of Thutmose I (1539-1514). The order to kill the Hebrew babies was given by a ruler of the 18th dynasty. Hatshepsut was the princess who adopted Moses, and Moses and Thutmose III (1452-1450) grew up as rivals in the court. Moreover, Thutmose III would have been the Pharaoh who oppressed the Hebrews and who dies during Moses' exile from Egypt; Moses and Aaron dealt with Amenhotep II; and the exodus of some 2,000,000 Hebrews occurred under Amenhotep (1450-1425)/(1441).

It may be remarked in passing that the fact that the Pharaohs of the 18th dynasty were Black may account for some of the anti-Black Biblical interpretation of the Jewish rabbis as set forth in the Talmud and Midrashim.

With References to Hebrews Having Been Brought Out of Egypt

By far the largest group of references of a single kind to Egypt in the Old Testament have to do with the Hebrews having been brought or led out of Egypt, one hundred thirty-five in number. These references appear in twenty of the thirty-nine books that make up the Old Testament. The largest number appears in the book of Exodus (31) followed by the second largest in the book of Deuteronomy (23). The rest of the

----

11. See liberal historians such as Bright, Jagersma, and Robinson, op. cit.

12. Wood, op. cit., pp. 83ff. Aling holds similar views.

Pentateuch, the books of Leviticus and Numbers, contain twenty. Other instances are contained in the historical books (37), the Psalms (4), and in seven of the prophetical books (20). In the main, the passages in which the references are located fall into three groups: those that assert the event as having taken place; those that are reminders of the event, and those that call for praise in remembrance of the event. On another hand, these references are in addition to numerous ones that refer back to the "mighty acts of God" performed in Egypt on behalf of the Hebrews.

In Prophetic Oracles

One hundred eighty-three times Egypt is referred to in eleven of the sixteen books of the prophets (including the book of Daniel). Primarily these references are in the form of oracles or are contained in oracles. However, some occur in or as historical accounts within some of the prophetical books. Still others consist only of allusions to Egypt. In descending numerical order the number of references are as follows: Jeremiah, 62; Ezekiel, 48; Isaiah, 37; Hosea, 13; Amos, 7; Zechariah, 5; Micah, 4; Daniel, 4; Joel, 1; Nahum, 1; and Haggai, 1.

In the ensuing presentation the chronological order in which the prophets lived, and presumably the dates when the various prophecies in the books, in the main, were delivered and/or written down are observed. It is to be noted that the historical periods ranged from around 760B.C to 164B.C.

The Book of Amos (760-750 B.C.). The references in Amos have to do with God's having brought the Hebrews out of Egypt, and with comparing the doom that is to befall Israel with that which had fallen upon Egypt (chapters 2:10, 3:1; 3:9; 4:10; 8:8; 9:5; 9:7).

The Book of Hosea (750-721 B.C.) Five types of oracles with reference to Egypt are to be found in the book of Hosea: that in which the prophet asserts that God has been Israel's God since the days of enslavement in Egypt; that which deals with God's having brought Israel out of Egypt; that in which the prophet harshly criticizes Israel for seeking Egypt's help; that in which the prophet declares that because of her sins Israel will return to Egypt; and that in which the prophet declares that because God cannot ultimately give her up she will return from Egypt (chapters 2:15; 7:11; 7:16; 8:13; 9:3; 11:1; 11:5; 11:11; 12:1; 12:9; 12:13; 13:4).

The Book of Isaiah, chapters 1-39 (742-682 B.C.). That portion of the book of Isaiah which is attributed to Isaiah ben Amoz, chapters 1-39 in the main, and which dates from 742 B.C. to 682 B.C., contains four important anti-Egyptian prophecies and one pro-Egyptian prophecy. The pro-Egyptian prophecy, however, may date from as late as the Hellenistic period (332-141 B.C. in Old Testament History).

The first anti-Egyptian oracle pronounces doom upon Egypt; it is contained in Chapter 19:1-17.[13] The second consists of a symbolic prophecy acted out by the prophet as for a period of three years (715-712 B.C.) he went about naked and barefoot. By his actions he proclaimed that Egypt (and Ethiopia) shall be led away as captives of war by the Assyrians, and stated that those who trust in the Egyptians and Ethiopians will be dismayed and confounded (Chapter 20). The third, which dates also as does the second from the period when the Ethiopian dynasty ruled Egypt, warns the people of Judah against going down to Egypt for help (chapter 30:1-18). Oracle number four among the anti-Egyptian prophecies, contained in chapter 31:1-3, repeats the message of the third.

The pro-Egyptian oracle (chapter 19:18-26) foresees a day when Israel's God will be worshipped in Egypt by the Egyptians, and when Egypt along with Israel and Assyria will be blessed.

The Book of Isaiah, chapters 40-55 (540 B.C.). Within the chapters of the book of Isaiah that are believed by numerous critical scholars to date from the period of the Babylonian exile (597-538 B.C.) are two oracles which refer to Egypt. The first of these (chapter 43:1-7) is a message of comfort for Judah, promising to give to Cyrus the Persian ruler Egypt (and Ethiopia along with Seba) as a ransom for the people of Judah in exile. The second (chapter 45:14-17) promises that the Egyptians (along with Ethiopians and Sabeans) will become subject to the Judahites and recognize their God.

The Book of Micah (735-700 B.C.). Micah's four references to Egypt have to do with God's having brought Israel out of Egypt; with the people of Assyria and Egypt coming to Judah; and with God's doing marvelous things as when Israel first came out of Egypt (chapters 6:4; 7:12; and 7:15).

The Book of Nahum (612-600 B.C.). Nahum's one reference to Egypt (chapter 3:8-9) equates the forthcoming

---

13. Ira Maurice Price, Ovid R. Sellers, and E. Leslie Carlson, *The Monuments and the Old Testament* (Philadelphia: The Judson Press, 1958), p. 282, state that Isaiah 19 describes the distress of Egypt under the Assyrians during the period of the Ethiopian dynasty.

destruction of Ninevah, capital of the Assyrian empire, with the fall of No-Amon (Thebes) which the prophet states fell despite aid from Egypt, Ethiopia, Put, and Lubim. The fall of Thebes occurred in 663 B.C., toward the end of the Twenty-fifth Ethiopian dynasty.

The Book of Jeremiah (626-582 B.C.). As noted above, the book of Jeremiah contains the greatest number of references to Egypt among the prophetical books, sixty-two. Within the book there are five prophecies directed against the Egyptians; one prophecy favorable to the Egyptians; two prophecies against the people of Judah some of whom have fled to Egypt; and five historical accounts that tell of events involving Egypt which occurred during and immediately after the last days of the Kingdom of Judah (609-582 B.C.). In the succeeding discussion the prophecies are dealt with; the historical accounts are treated under the next caption.

The first anti-Egyptian prophecy (chapter 2:14-37) upbraids the people of Judah for having trusted in Egypt (and Assyria) instead of having trusted in God, and prophesies that they shall be put to shame by the Egyptians even as they had been by the Assyrians. The second (chapter 9:25f.) includes Egypt among other "uncircumcised" peoples who are to be punished by God. In chapter 43:8-13 the third anti-Egyptian oracle, spoken by Jeremiah in the Egyptian city of Tahpanhes, proclaims doom upon the Pharaoh and upon Egypt. Anti-Egyptian oracle number four prophecies an ill fate for Pharaoh Hophra (chapter 44:30). And the fifth, which consists of the whole of chapter 46 except for part of one verse, pronounces doom upon Egypt and Pharaoh Necho at the hands of Nebuchadnezzar, King of Babylon. This prophecy did come true when in 586 the Babylonian ruler did invade Egypt. The prophecy favorable for the Egyptians is composed of verse 26b, chapter 46. It states that after Egypt's destruction by Nebuchadnezzar the country shall be inhabited as in olden times.

Chapters 24:8-10 and 44:1-29 contain the anti-Judahite oracles. The objects of the oracles are those people of Judah who remain in Canaan; and those who have fled to Egypt, now living in the Egyptian cities of Migdol, Tahpanhes, Memphis, and in the land of Pathros (Upper Egypt) because they now serve other gods.

The Book of Ezekiel (593-570 B.C.). The forty-eight references to Egypt in the book of Ezekiel are distributed among three types of prophecies. Those of the first type are pronounced against the people of Judah because they are seeking help from

Egypt or because the ancestors committed idolatry during the period of Egyptian enslavement. The second type, consisting of the whole of chapters 29-32, primarily, is directed against Egypt. The third type, represented only by one brief oracle hidden away in chapter 29:13-16, prophesies restoration of Egypt after a period of forty years, albeit as a very powerless nation that recognizes the Lord as God.

An oracle in chapter 17:11-21 adversely criticizes the King of Judah for sending ambassadors to Egypt for help against the King of Babylon. Chapter 19 consists of a lament over former King Jehoahaz who had been taken captive by Pharaoh Necho to Egypt in the year 609 B.C. (See also II Kings 23:30-34, duplicated in II Chronicles 36:1-4). In chapter 20 appears an oracular reply by the prophet to certain of the elders of the Judahite people in Babylonian exile who came to inquire of the Lord. Ezekiel states that God would have destroyed the fathers for their idolatry in Egypt but for his name's sake. And in chapter 23 the prophet castigates the people of Judah for having (allegorically) committed adultery with the Egyptians formerly as well as presently.

As noted, the whole of chapters 29-32 consists of prophecies concerning Egypt, all of which except one are anti-Egyptian. In these, Egypt's coming destruction by Nebuchadnezzar is predicted which prediction came to reality[14] as we have noted in 568 B.C., under reference to Jeremiah, chapter 46.

The Book of Haggai (520 B.C.). Haggai's one reference to Egypt (chapter 2:5) reminds the people of the restored Judahite community in Jerusalem of the covenant made with them (the fathers) when they came out of Egypt.

The Book of Joel (ca. 350 B.C.). Joel's prophecy, contained in chapter 3:19, and anti-Egyptian, asserts that Egypt (along with Edom) will become desolate because of violence done to Judah.

The Book of Zechariah (ca. 300-200 B.C.). The five references to Egypt in the book of Zechariah appear in those sections of the book that most critical scholars date in the Hellenistic period (332-164 B.C.). They occur in two kinds of

----

14. In passing, it may be noted that these prophecies of Ezekiel, all dated between 587-570 B.C., serve as an excellent historical commentary on the glory of ancient Egypt and Ethiopia, and on Egypt's origins in the South. Further, they serve as a good theological commentary on Egypt from a Judahite point of view. Further still they set forth an exact prediction of Egypt's future as it will become under the Persians and others.

passages that hold out hope for the Jews. In the first it is prophesied that Jewish exiles shall be brought back from the land of Egypt while at the same time Egypt's power will be eliminated (chapter 10:10-11). The second states that a plague will come upon the Egyptians if they fail to come up to Jerusalem in order to observe the Feast of Booths (chapter 14:18-19).

The Book of Daniel (165-164 B.C.). In chapter 11 of the book of Daniel several verses which make reference to Egypt are to be found. According to critical literary-historical scholars, verse 8 refers to Ptolemy III who captured the fortress of Seleucia and brought back much booty to Egypt. Further, verse 9 is said to have reference to the king and country of Egypt. Verses 40-45 predict that Ptolemy will provoke a war in which Antiochus, the Seleucid ruler, will conquer Libya, Egypt, and Ethiopia, but will perish along the seacoast.

Egypt in Historical Relations with Israelites-Judahites-Jews

This topic has both an exclusive and an inclusive peculiarity. It excludes what some regard as historical accounts in the narratives concerning the patriarchs and Joseph, and of the enslavement, Moses, and the exodus—all of which are found in the Law books. It deals with the data in the "historical" books. Further, it does not include some forty-four references to Egypt in the books of Joshua, Judges, and Samuel which, for the most part, refer to the enslavement in and exodus from Egypt. On the other hand, the topic does include data of a historical nature found in some of the prophetical books as noted above. In some cases this latter material duplicates information given in the historical books; in others it supplements, as is indicated.

In toto, there are one hundred eighteen references to Egypt in the historical books. Those in the books of I and II Kings (including duplicate passages in II Chronicles, Isaiah, and Jeremiah) deal with nine matters, as follows: (1) the marriage of Solomon to the daughter of a Pharaoh (I Kings 3:1; 9:16); (2) Solomon's trade with Egypt in horses and chariots (I Kings 10:28f., duplicated in II Chronicles 1:16f.; 9:28); (3) Hadad the Edomite's flight to Egypt from David, reception by the King of Egypt who gave him a sister-in-law for wife, and Hadad's return to Edom after David's death (I Kings 11:17-21); (4) Jeroboam the Ephraimite's flight to Egypt from Solomon where he remained under the protection of Pharaoh Shishak until Solomon's death whereupon he returned to Israel (I Kings

11:40f., 12:1ff., duplicated in II Chronicles 10:2); (5) Shishak's invasion of Judah and placing it under tribute (I Kings 14:25, expanded in II Chronicles 12:2-9); (6) Hoshea King of Israel's seeking help from So (?) King of Egypt against the Assyrians (II Kings 17:4); (7) The Chaldean Rabshekah's speech to the people of Judah about their unwise reliance upon Egypt for help (II Kings 18:21ff., duplicated in Isaiah, chapter 36); (8) Egypt's domination of Judah by Pharaoh Necho, including Necho's defeat of King Josiah, his dethronement of King Jehoahaz, and his installation of Jehoiakim as King of Judah, during the period 609-605 B.C. (II Kings 23:29-24-7, duplicated and expanded in II Chronicles 35:20-36:4); and (9) Flight of Judahite refugees to Egypt (II Kings 25:26, expanded in Jeremiah 43:1ff.). An additional historical reference appears in Jeremiah, chapter 37:5-7. It reports the coming of an Egyptian army to assist Judah against the Chaldeans, and the prophet's prediction that the army is about to return to Egypt.

In regard to Solomon's marriage to an Egyptian princess it is notable that of his reputed seven hundred wives and three hundred concubines she is the chieftess. More is said about her than about all the others. It is more than interesting to note that the author of II Chronicles (chapter 8:11) makes the following statement concerning her, in addition to what is stated in II Kings, "and Solomon brought up the daughter of Pharaoh out of the city of David unto the house that he had built for her; for he said, my wife shall not dwell in the house of David King of Israel, because the places are holy, where unto the ark of the Lord hath come."[15]

Scholars variously assess the significance of the marriage and of the capture of the city of Gezer by the Pharaoh who gave it to Solomon as a dowry for the princess. One view holds that the marriage indicates the superiority of Solomon's empire over the Egyptian kingdom of that time.[16] Another sees the capture of Gezer by the Pharaoh as an attempt to reassert Egyptian power in Asia.[17] In addition there are questions in regard to the identity of the Pharaoh. It seems clear that he was a ruler during the Twenty-First dynasty (1090-940 B.C.). Some scholars believe

---

15. The Chronicler, writing between 400-250 B.C., thinks that this *Hamite* would contaminate both the dynasty of David and the holy places.

16. For a contrary view, see Robinson, op. cit., p. 246, and Unger op. cit., p. 221. Frank, op. cit., p. 164 and Bright, op. cit., p. 212, support the view.

17. See Bright, op. cit., and Frank, op. cit.

that he was not a Pharaoh over all Egypt, but merely a prince who ruled in the eastern Delta region. On the other hand there are those who identify him with Psusennes II (ca. 984-950 B.C.);[18] while still others identify him with Siamun, next to the last of the Twenty-First dynasty rulers (ca. 976-958 B.C.).[19] Solomon's trade in horses and chariots between Egypt and Asia Minor is confirmed by archaeology.

The flight to Egypt by Hadad the Edomite during David's reign and that of Jeroboam during the reign of Solomon shows that Egypt was a haven of safety and support for adversaries of Judah during those times. It appears that the Pharaoh of Hadad's day sought to discourage his return to Edom in order to reassert independence from Judah during the time of Solomon.[20] On the other hand, Shishak (Sheshonk) founder of the Twenty-Second dynasty (940-745 B.C.) might well have given encouragement to Jeroboam toward the end of weakening Judah.[21] The preceding conjecture is supported by the fact that in the fifth year of Rehoboam's reign Shishak invaded Judah and forced her to pay tribute. This invasion is attested by Shishak's own record which is engraved on a pylon that he erected at the temple of Karnak. This record indicates that he invaded not only the Kingdom of Judah but that of Israel as well; and represents a reassertion of Egyptian power in Asia.[22]

The reference to King Hoshea's seeking help from So, King of Egypt, against the Assyrians makes for a number of problems. Chief among these is the identity of So. Some view the name as being that of a Pharaoh, variously identified with Sibe, a petty king of the East Delta;[23] with Seve or Shabaka who at the time was a commander of Egyptian forces under his father

----

18. Frank, op. cit.

19. See Bright, op. cit., p. 212; Aling, op. cit., p. 121; Siegfried Hermann, *A History of Israel in Old Testament Times*, trans. by John Bowden from the German (Philadelphia: Fortress Press, 1975), p. 183 and others.

20. Frank, op. cit.

21. Ibid.

22. See, George A. Barton, *Archaeology and the Bible* (7th ed. Philadelphia: American Sunday School Union, 1937), pp. 28, 456f., and others.

23. Price et al., op. cit., pp. 261f.

Pianki;[24] or probably Tefnakhte of the Twenty-Fourth dynasty.[25] Others see the name as referring to a place: thus So is taken to be the Hebrew rendering of the Egyptian word Sais,[26] Marcel Taperruque of France in "La Bible Et Les Civilizations Du Nil" is among those who claim that So cannot be identified.[27]

Concerning Pharaoh Necho II's domination of Judah, this lasted only during the period 609-605 B.C. After 605, as the Bible indicates (II Kings 24:7), the Egyptian ruler did not come out of his land, for the King of Babylon had taken from the River of Egypt unto the River Euphrates all that pertained to the King of Egypt.

In Poetical-Wisdom Literature

Within the poetical-wisdom books of the Old Testament are six references to Egypt of great significance. The first of these appears in Psalm 68:31 where it is declared (according to the King James Version translation) that princes shall come out of Egypt. In four passages (Psalms 78:51; 105:23, 27; and 106:21f.) Egypt poetically is called the "land of Ham." The sixth reference is in Proverbs 7:16 wherein advice is given to a young man against consorting with an adulteress who has decked her bed "with fine linen from Egypt."

ETHIOPIA/CUSH

As a Term of Identification

Four times the word "Cush" appears in the Old Testament as the name of a person (Genesis 10:6, 7, 8, duplicated in I Chronicles 1:8, 9, 10; and Psalm 7). In the first three instances the person is stated to be the first son of Ham, one of Noah's three sons, the (eponymous) ancestor of various peoples located

---

24. See Elmer W. K. Mould, *Essentials of Bible History* (rev. ed. New York: Ronald Press Company, 1951), p.251. In agreement with Mould is E. Mveng, "La Bible Et L' Afrique Noire," in *Black Africa and The Bible*, ed. by E. Mveng and R.J.Z. Werblowsky (New York: Anti-Defamation League of B'nai B'rith, 1972). Mveng refers to Shabaka as the Black founder of the Twenty-Fifth dynasty.

25. Bright, p. 275.

26. Ibid.

27. Mveng and Werblowsky, op. cit.

in Africa and Southwest Asia, and the particular father of Nimrod who founded cities in Mesopotamia. In the fourth it appears as the name of a Benjaminite in the title of the Psalm.

In the form of "Cushite" the word appears twice in Numbers 12:1 as the identifying characteristic of a woman whom Moses is said to have married. This designation is applied again in Jeremiah 38:7, 10, 12, where Ebed-Melech, an officer in King Jehoiakim's court, is described as being an Ethiopian, or as it is in Hebrew a Cushite. And in II Samuel 18:21-32 the designation "The Cushite" (Cushite with the definite article) is applied eight times to a courier in David's army. "Cushi" as the name of a person appears once in Jeremiah 36:14ff. where it is given as the name of the great-grandfather of Jehudi, another member of King Jehoiakim's court. The name appears a second time in Zephaniah 1:1 wherein it is stated that a person of that name was the father of the prophet and a descendant of one Hezekiah, presumably a former king of Judah and therefore a member of the dynasty of David.

With references to Moses' having married a Cushite woman, White scholars generally, liberal and conservative, may take passing notice but never make inferences relative to a Black component within the ancient Hebrew populace.[28] Some attempt to explain the reference away as having nothing to do with a Black person, as did the ancient Jewish rabbis who interpreted the passage symbolically. It was upon the basis of the rabbinical interpretation rather than the Bible itself that Cecil B. DeMille in the movie "The Ten Commandments" could portray Moses' wife as White.[29] Taking the Biblical text at face value, and even ignoring Josephus' report that Moses married an Ethiopian princess,[30] the passage can be harmonized with Zipporah's, though a Midianite, having been the wife referred to. Cushites lived in Arabia and elsewhere in Asia as well as in Africa.

The presence of a Cushite in David's mercenary army (II Samuel 18:21-32) led H. Preserved Smith in his commentary on "The Books of Samuel" to refer to him as a "negro" who was

---

28. An exception is Merrill F. Unger, op. cit., p. 136. For a Black African scholar's apt discussion of the subject one should see E. Mveng's article cited above.

29. See Henry S. Noerdlinger, *Moses and Egypt* (Los Angeles: University of Southern California Press, 1956), p. 70 for a discussion.

30. See *The Works of Flavius Josephus*, translated by William Whiston, A.M. (Hartford, Conn.: S.S. Scranton Co., 1903), "Antiquities of the Jews," Book II chapter X, p. 76.

"naturally a slave."[31] A far better description lies in the fact that David employed Philistine mercenaries who had come from Crete where Black troops had been in service since early Minoan times, having come from Ethiopia and Egypt.[32]

Ebed-Melech (Jeremiah 36:14ff.) and Jehudi, great-grandson of one Cushi (Jeremiah 38:7ff.) demand great attention. Interestingly and strangely only one White scholar of whom I am aware has mentioned them as members of the Judahite court during Jeremiah's time. This scholar, H. Jagersma, in his recent history of Israel, directs the reader to an article published in Howard University's *Journal of Religious Thought*, and written by Professor G. Rice of Howard on "Two Black Contemporaries of Jeremiah."[33]

As a Geographical Reference

Six times Ethiopia/Cush appears as a place name for an apparently distant land located in some instances south of Egypt. In Genesis 2:13 it is given as the name of a place around which the River Gihon flows. Twice in the book of Esther (chapters 1:1 and 8:9) the name appears as one of two extreme boundaries of the Persian empire. In Isaiah 18:1 reference is made to a land that lies beyond the rivers of Ethiopia and that sends ambassadors by the Nile. The prophet Ezekiel pronounces doom upon Egypt that shall reach to the border of Ethiopia (chapter 29:10); and in II Chronicles 21:16 an invasion of Judah by Arabians who live near the Ethiopians is reported.

In Prophetic Oracles

Ethiopia/Cush is referred to in prophetic oracles within the books of Isaiah, Jeremiah, Ezekiel, Daniel, Amos, Nahum, and Zephaniah. Herein the references are dealt with according to the chronological order of the prophet's appearance in history

---

31. Henry Preserved Smith, *The Books of Samuel*, Vol VIII of *The International Critical Commentary*, ed. by Charles Agustus Briggs, Samuel Rolles Driver, and Alfred Plummer (New York: Charles Scribner's Sons, 1899), p. 359.

32. See Harrison, op. cit., for an Egyptian origin of Minoan Cretan civilization; and especially Joseph E. Harris, ed., *Africa and Africans as Seen by Classical Writers: The William Leo Hansberry African History Notebook*, Vol. II (Washington, D.C.: Howard University Press, 1977), p. 136.

33. H. Jagersma, op. cit., p. 175.

except in the case of two passages in the book of Isaiah, and in the case of the prophet and book of Daniel.

The Book of Amos (*760-750 B.C.*). In Amos (chapter 9:7) the prophet compares the Israelites to the Ethiopians, stating that they are equal in God's sight.

The Book of Isaiah (*742-682 B.C.; 540 B.C.*). In Isaiah (chapter 20) Ethiopia is included with Egypt as the object of a prophecy of doom, as was noted in the discussion under Egypt.

From a later date, around 540 B.C., are two oracles which appear in the so-called Second Isaiah (chapters 43:3 and 45:14). Again, as noted in the discussion under Egypt, the passage in which the first of the verses appears contains a message of hope for Judahite exiles. According to it Ethiopia (along with Egypt and Seba) will be given in ransom for them. And still again as was noted in the discussion under Egypt, verse 14 of chapter 45 appears in a prophecy that predicts subservience of Ethiopia, Egypt, and the Sabeans to the restored people of Judah.

The Book of Zephaniah (*626 B.C.*). Zephaniah contains two references to Ethiopia: one in an oracle that states the destruction of Ethiopia along with several other nations (chapter 2:12), and one in an oracle that foresees the time when worshipers of God who lived beyond the rivers of Ethiopia will bring offerings to Jerusalem (chapter 3:10). The latter passage may refer to Judahites in dispersion or to native Africans who will be converted to Israel's religion.

The Book of Jeremiah (*626-582 B.C.*). In chapter 13:23 the prophet uses the unchangebility of the Ethiopian's color to argue that the people of Judah cannot change their sinful ways, while in chapter 39:15-18 he pronounces a blessing upon Ebed-Melech the Ethiopian because he trusted in God. And in chapter 46:9 the prophet includes the Ethiopians among the peoples who had been helpless in aiding the Egyptians against the Chaldeans in the Battle of Carchemish (605 B.C.).

The Book of Nahum (*612-600 B.C.*). As noted in the discussion under Egypt, the one reference to Ethiopia in the book of Nahum (chapter 3:9) includes Ethiopia as one of the countries that supported the Egyptian city of Thebes but were unable to prevent its fall in 663 B.C. to the Assyrians.

The Book of Ezekiel (*593-570 B.C.*). An oracle of doom pronounced primarily upon Egypt in chapter 30 includes Ethiopia three times as being also the object of destruction (verses 4, 5, and 9); and in chapter 38:5 Ethiopia is included among several nations that the prophet says shall be destroyed.

The Book of Daniel (*165/164 B.C.*) Chapter 11:43 includes the Ethiopians among those whom Antiochus will conquer, as noted in the discussion under Egypt.

Ethiopia/Cush in Historical Relations with Judahites

With the inclusion of the account of the Queen of Sheba's visit with Solomon (I Kings 10:1-10, 13, duplicated in II Chronicles 9:1-10, 12), and of the reference to Ophir in I Kings 10:11-12 duplicated in II Chronicles 9:10-11, there are possibly six instances in which Ethiopia/Cush appears in historical relations with the Kingdom of Judah. That of the Queen's visit would chronologically be the first, while the reference to Solomon's trade with Ophir would be the second, both occurring during Solomon's reign, roughly 960-922 B.C. The third instance is recorded in II Chronicles 12:13 wherein it is reported that Ethiopians were in the army of Shishak, the Pharaoh who invaded Judah during the reign of King Rehoboam, already referred to under the discussion of Egypt. (See also I Kings 14:25-26 in which passage there is no reference to Ethiopians in Shishak's army.) The next two references to Ethiopia/Cush are given only in II Chronicles (chapter 14:9-15 and 16:8) wherein the author states that there was an invasion of Judah by one Zerah the Ethiopian who was defeated by King Asa (913-873 B.C.). The sixth instance occurs with reference to Tirhakah (Taharqua) (II Kings 19:9, duplicated in Isaiah 37:9, but not mentioned in II Chronicles) who is said to be king of Ethiopia and who is coming to assist Judah against the Assyrians.

Relative to the visit of the Queen of Sheba with Solomon, Edward Ullendorff in his volume *Ethiopia and The Bible* regards the event as historical and locates Sheba in either Southwest Arabia or the Horn of Africa.[34] Josephus in his *Antiquities* states that she was Queen of Ethiopia and Egypt, Ethiopia referring to the land immediately south of Egypt, centered in Meroe.[35] On the other hand, the author of "Black Heroes in World History," (*Biographies From Tuesday Magazine*) regards the Queen as having her capital in Axum (Abyssinia or modern Ethiopia), but with her kingdom including Southwest Arabia.[36] With this view

----

34. Edward Ullendorff, op. cit. (London: Oxford University Press, 1968), pp. 130ff.

35. Op. cit., Book VIII, Chapter VI, p. 253.

36. Op. cit., p.2.

William Leo Hansberry was in agreement, upon the basis of his notes edited by Joseph E. Harris,[37] as is the Reverend Jacob A. Dyer in his booklet, *The Ethiopian in the Bible*.[38]

Father Mveng of the Cameroun argues that the Queen is to be identified as the Queen of Saba which in (most) ancient times, going back to the Twelfth dynasty in Egypt (1991-1786 B.C.) was the capital of the Kingdom of Cush, and that Saba is to be identified with Meroe.[39]

Whether Ophir, with which land Solomon traded should be included in this essay is debatable. Leon Wood notes that four different locations have been suggested only one of which is in Africa: Southwest Arabia, Southeast Arabia, Somaliland, and Supara in India.[40] To these four must be added a location established by Father Mveng, namely the region of Zimbabwe[41] —a location that perhaps would take the land out of boundaries of Ancient Ethiopia. Outstanding scholars among the liberal Biblical historians opt in favor of Somaliland.[42] Unger decides on modern day Yemen and the African coast,[43] while Wood favors India.[44]

The identity of Zerah, the Ethiopian, makes for still another problem in history. As Keita Tarharka Sundiata notes in his book, *Black Manhood: The Building of Civilization by the Black Man of The Nile*, Zerah was identified by Jean F. Champollion with Osorkon I, second King of the Twenty-second dynasty, (ca. 914-874).[45] This view has now been largely abandoned. Professor Harry M. Orlinsky regards him as head of an Egyptian army,[46] then as the probable leader of Arabian

---

37. Joseph E. Harris, ed., *Pillars in Ethiopian History: The William Leo Hansberry African History Notebook*, Vol. 1 (Washington, D.C.: Howard University Press, 1974), p. 59.

38. Op. cit., (New York, Washington, Hollywood: Vantage Press, 1974), pp. 27ff.

39. Op. cit., p.28.

40. Op. cit., p. 292.

41. Op. cit., p. 27.

42. For example, William Foxwell Albright, *Archaeology and the Religion of Israel* (New York: Doubleday and Company, Inc., 1969), p. 130; Bright, op. cit., p. 215; Frank, op. cit., p. 138.

43. Op. cit., p. 225.

44. Op. cit., p. 292.

45. Op. cit., (Washington, D.C.: University Press of America, 1979), p. 272.

46. *In Ancient Israel* (Ithaca, New York: Cornell University Press, 1954), p. 103.

Bedouin tribes.[47] John Bright thinks that he might have been a commander of Egyptian mercenary troops left behind by Shishak.[48] In substantial agreement with Bright is Leon Wood who regards Zerah as an Ethiopian, likely a military leader under Osorkon I.[49] Closely akin to Orlinsky's latter view is that of J.M. Meyers who thinks that he may have been an Ethiopian, or an Arabian from Cushan who was an adventurer in the Pharaoh's pay.[50]

In Poetical-Wisdom Literature

Ethiopia is referred to three times in the poetical-wisdom literature of the Old Testament: in Job 29:19 where reference is made to the topaz of Ethiopia; in Psalm 68:31 which states that Ethiopia shall soon stretch out her hands unto God; and in Psalm 87:4 where Ethiopia is mentioned along with other places of renown.

SUMMARY OBSERVATIONS

The foregoing study discloses that Egypt and Ethiopia figure in the most ancient traditions, and in the literature of the Hebrews-Israelites-Judahites-Jews from all periods of the Old Testament history. It reveals further that the two countries, especially Egypt, are referred to in a majority of the books that constitute the Protestant Old Testament. It notes that almost without exception the references to the two countries are negative in nature. Apart from the few pro-Egyptian/Ethiopian passages that were noted, and a passage in Deuteronomy 23:7 wherein it is stated that you are not to abhor an Egyptian because you were a sojourner in his land, there is hardly anything good said about either country.

Further still, the study demonstrates that Egypt was involved in Old Testament history from earliest times, and that

---

47. *In Understanding the Bible Through History and Archaeology* (New York: Ktav Publishing House, Inc., 1972), p. 177.

48. Op. cit., p. 235.

49. Op. cit., p.341f.

50. Reported by Bright, op. cit.,p. 235.

Ethiopia figured in that same history from the beginning of the Twenty-fifth, Ethiopian dynasty.

That of the some seven hundred forty references to Egypt most are in the main of a negative nature should be no surprise. How could it be otherwise, considering the fact that the Egyptians were the oppressors, and the memory of Egyptian oppression was kept alive throughout the generations. Yet, an ambivalent love-hate relationship with or attitude toward Egypt existed throughout Old Testament history. Egypt, across the years, was a haven of refuge, so that even in New Testament times the author of the Gospel according to Matthew could tell of Jesus' escape to Egypt, then use Hosea 11:1 as a reference to Jesus' return from the land.

Chapter 5

African Americans and Biblical Hermeneutics

Black Interpretation of The Bible

Dr. Waters, and other colleagues, I stand before you as one who has lived and lives halfway between two generations of Black critical Biblical scholarship: between the first generation represented by such personalities as the late Bishop Benjamin Tucker Tanner who in reaction against the then just come-of-age historical-literary Biblical criticism and its either elimination of Black peoples from the Bible or denigration of the few Biblical characters that it decided were Black, wrote his *The Color of Solomon What?* and *The Negro in Holy Writ*; and between you of the present generation. Those among the older generation were novices and with meager foundations; I was and am of mediocre foundation; you have a most solid foundation and are equipped to engage in the best of scholarly pursuits. I take the opportunity here provided to pay tribute to the elders, and to salute you, my superiors.

The subject that was presented to me, as you note on the program, is "African Americans and Biblical Hermeneutics." As the subject was explained to me, it has to do with Black interpretation of the Bible. When I inquired about what I was expected to do with the subject, I was told, "Just do anything that you want to do; say anything that you want to say."

Well, not being an expert in the area, I decided to go to those who have demonstrated expertise, especially during the past fifteen years, and to present what I could find among their contributions. In searching among the many writings of Black theologians and Biblical scholars, I did uncover a few instances of what I regard to be significant statements that say something about the subject at hand.

Among Biblical scholars whose works I have examined, those of Henry H. Mitchell; the Reverend William Mason, who at the time of his contribution was minister of the Central Reformed Church of Paterson, New Jersey; the late Bishop Joseph A. Johnson, Jr; James Cone; Major J. Jones; and Father Robert A. Bennett, have proved helpful. Much to my regret I was unable to find anything from or by Carl H. Marbury apart from an outline of a course that he offered in a winter quarter, 1973, entitled "Biblical Interpretation and Black Theology." It may be that others such as Dave Shannon have made contributions to the subject of which I was unaware. For my ignorance I offer an apology.

First, I shall present findings that have to do with "hermeneutic" in relation to African Americans. Next I shall report on "hermeneutics," viewed as dealing with principles of Biblical interpretation employed by African Americans. Thirdly, I shall deal with discoveries that treat of "hermeneutic" and "hermeneutics" in combination. And, lastly, inasmuch as I have the privilege of "saying anything that I want to say." I shall give some reactions. As we go along, you will note that the terms "hermeneutic" and "hermeneutics" are not always used consistently. Further, I shall quote from and paraphrase from my authors using their grammar and sentence structure.

The Reverend Dr. Robert A. Bennett informs us that the term "hemeneutic" means to translate, to transmit, and to interpret. On this subject, from the Black perspective, hardly anyone has had more to say than Dr. Henry H. Mitchell. The very first chapter in his book *Black Preaching* carries the title "Why Hermeneutic?" In this first chapter he suggests that the Black "hermeneutic" is parallel to the new "hermeneutic" of Ebeling and others, yet not legitimatized by the same criteria. Continuing, he states, "If the chief task of "hermeneutics" [*sic*] is to convey the revelation [of God] in its contemporary context, then Black "hermeneutics" [*sic*] far outstrips this school, which most Blacks never heard of anyway." Before informing the reader that he has used the term "hermeneutic" as a code word for putting the gospel on a tell-it-like-it-is, nitty-gritty basis, he asserts that the Black "hermeneutic" must seek to look into the message of the Black past and see what the Black Fathers could be saying to Black people today. In a later chapter he identifies the Black Fathers partly as those Black pastors serving in Black churches which were primarily under Black control, from the late eighteenth century to the early twentieth century. The term included early freeborn preachers, slave preachers, and those who, like Richard Allen, were able to purchase their freedom. First of all, they were interpreters of the Bible and of religious truth, and their interpretations were designed to meet the needs of Black people in a hostile white world.

Along with statements such as the foregoing, back in chapter one of his book, Henry spells out what he calls two very sound principles advanced by the "new hermeneutic" school of thought—rules [sic] followed by the Black Fathers long before the "new hermeneutic" was spelled out. These "rules" are: first, one must declare the gospel in the language and culture of the people—the vernacular; second (using the word principle instead of rule) the gospel must speak to the contemporary man and his needs.

In agreement with Mitchell, at least with respect to an association of the "new hermeneutic" with the Black experience, is the Reverend William Mason. In an article entitled "Hermeneutics and the Black Experience," and published in the *Reformed Review* (Summer 1970, Vol. 23/No. 4), Mr. Mason informs the reader that sometimes the word hermeneutics is used synonymously with the word exegesis which has to do with the meaning of a particular text, but has come to apply more to the study of laws and principles of interpretation in general. He states the main issue of this paper to be: "The relationship that hermeneutics has to imparting the word to people of the black experience in America." His focus lies in the development of three basic assumptions which, worded somewhat differently in parts of the paper, are: 1) There was and still is a black hermeneutic and it has great significance to the study of hermeneutics; 2) The black experience in America has significance for the study of hermeneutics; and 3) Preaching has been the cornerstone of the Christian education of black people.

"Classical hermeneutics, as presented by the historical critical school, does not speak to the condition of the black man in America as does the new hermeneutic," he goes on to say. He then raises a question, "Could it be that the new hermeneutic of

Ebeling and Fuchs is an extension of the black hermeneutic?" Moreover, Black preaching which embodied the Black hermeneutic was not preaching based on a keen exegesis of Scripture.

In his concluding paragraph, Mr. Mason states: "It is the black preacher and the black mother, steeped in the true meaning of Christian nurture, who have been God's leading hermeneutical agents in America. What they have said has been in the style of symbolic and poetic modes of thought. The validity of this style as a medium of God's revelation has been the work of form and literary critics. The black hermeneutical agent caught a glimpse of the new hermeneutic before it was academically formalized and in so doing, gave validity to the assumptions of this paper."

It is almost a natural act to move from what Messrs. Mitchell and Mason have written to the writings of the late Bishop Joseph A. Johnson, Jr., who was both a Biblical scholar and theologian, particularly to his book, *Proclamation Theology*. Chapter II of this book entitled "The Black Preacher and Proclamation Theology" deals with hermeneutics. After discussing the word hermeneutics at some length Bishop Johnson states:

> One may summarize this section of hermeneutics as follows. Hermeneutics is exegesis, commentary, translation, interpretation, self-understanding, text, interrogation and language. It is Fuch's definition of hermeneutics as `translation into language that speaks today' that makes possible the transition to a discussion of hermeneutics as wrestling with the will and word of God.

Under a discussion of "The Black Preacher and His Bible," the Bishop reports that he inquired of his father, a minister with only a seventh grade education, about his methodology or the steps involved in wrestling with the Scriptures. In reply, his father gave an answer which the Bishop himself formalized in twelve steps, as follows: "1) Prepare yourself with devotion and prayer prior to your encounter with the Scriptures. 2) Read the entire Book in which the text is located. 3) Become acquainted with all of the stories which lead up to the text and those that follow. 4) What were the problems, the situation of the participants in the story? 5) Read the biblical passages aloud, so as to hear the Scriptures and permit them to speak to you. 6) Discover the human element and the Divine element in the situation. 7) You must see what the writer saw, feel what the participants in the story felt and hear what they heard. 8) Use your imagination and put yourself in the place of the writer and participants of the story. 9) Assume the different roles of the principal characters in the story and act as if you were present when the story was first told. 10) Ask yourself this question, 'What special message does this passage of Scripture bring to your people for their healing and renewal?' 11) Then wait for God to speak. 12) When you preach, go slow, rise high, strike fire and sit down..."

From this presentation of his father's methodology, Bishop Johnson goes on to discuss "The Principles of Hermeneutics in the Black Tradition." Under this topic he includes the two principles enunciated by Mitchell, and already noted; then appears to adopt two principles enunciated by James Cone, namely: "The Christian understanding of God arises from the biblical view of revelation, a revelation of God that takes place in the liberation of oppressed Israel and is completed in His becoming man in Jesus Christ," and "The doctrine of God in Black theology must be God participating in the oppressed of the land. (Cone does, as Bishop Johnson indicates, state these two principles under the caption of "Hermeneutical Principle for the Doctrine of God," albeit in an expanded form, in his book *A Black Theology of Liberation*, pages 114ff.)

However, Bishop Johnson goes on to state:

> Needless to say that the hermeneutical principles of Black theology of James Cone and of *Black Preaching* by Henry Mitchell deserve special attention and actual critical study. Henry Mitchell's *Black Preaching* is highly recommended to any person who would seek to understand the hermeneutics which have developed consciously and unconsciously in the Black preaching tradition.

Bishop Johnson continues by stating his own hermeneutical principles, four in number, as follows:

> 1) The Christian gospel must be proclaimed in a vernacular of the people and the commentary on Scripture must come out of the Black experience.
> 2) God is the creator, sustainer, redeemer of the world and man and he actively is engaged in the work of liberation.

3) Jesus Christ is the revelation of the power, wisdom, and love of God. He is actively engaged in a ministry of healing, liberation and reconciliation.

4) The life, ministry, death and resurrection of Jesus has radically transformed the human situation and has made possible triumphant Christian living.

Reference to Jim Cone's hermeneutical principles in regard to the doctrine of God, by Bishop Johnson, leads one to Jim's own statement of what "the" hermeneutical principle to be employed in Biblical interpretation really is. In his book *God of The Oppressed*, under the caption of "Christian Theology and the Biblical Story," he writes:

> The hermeneutical principle for an exegesis of the Scriptures is the revelation of God in Christ as the Liberator of the oppressed from social oppression and to political struggle, wherein the poor recognize their fight against poverty and injustice is not only consistent with the gospel but is the gospel of Jesus Christ.

This pronouncement of James Cone led Bishop Johnson to complete agreement with many ideas, expressed by Dr. J. Deotis Roberts in his criticism of Cone as stated in an article, "A Critique of James H. Cone's *God of the Oppressed*." And after asserting his agreement, the Bishop goes on to say, "In his work Cone reveals a remarkable weakness in Biblical exegesis."

This criticism of Cone by Bishop Johnson is similar to one stated by Dr. Major J. Jones in a paper read before a seminar on "Black Theologians and the Bible," on November 21, 1975. Prior to making the criticism, Major stated under the heading of "The Use of the Bible as Proof-texting":

> ...there is tendency, on the part of many Black Theologians, to employ the Bible as a mere proof text to support many of their already pre-conceived ideas or points of views.... .When texts or passages of Scripture are taken out of context to prove one's own preconceived ideas, the Bible is not being properly interpreted....

Then, under the heading "Literalism as a Methodology," Dr. Jones goes on to say,

> ...there are few among Black Theologians who employ a legalistic literalism that fixes on the 'mere words of Scripture' to the almost total exclusion of meaning of the mere word or words; thus, making a correct understanding of the full meaning of Scripture all but impossible. It is not quite the same as a so-called belief in the Bible from cover-to-cover, or the Bible as the infallible book of God's word. However, it is just as strange.

From these comments, Major moves to what he calls "The Proper Objective Use of the Bible," under which caption he includes four things necessary for the practice of hermeneutics: 1) History and Culture, 2) Geography, 3) Religious Development, and 4) Context.

"Finally," he says,

> Black Theology should and must employ all of the elements involved in the interpretation of the Scripture, when it employs the Scripture—i.e., the text, the interpreter, the interpretation, and the rules governing interpretation—hermeneutics in its classical forms concentrates on the last. Under the inspiration of Bultmann, the existential dimension was added to the historical method; thus: hermeneutic came to embrace all of the elements involved in the interpretation of the Scripture.

Still further, after referring to his own book, *Christian Ethics for Black Theology* as a model for careful interpretation of Scripture for what it might say to contemporary issues, he gives his criticism of Cone. He states: "James Cone's *God of the Oppressed* represents another use. I view his use as very near proof-texting. The line is thin because of his prior views."

Jim Cone's statement of a principle for Biblical hermeneutics, and Major's comments may be viewed as a transition from hermeneutic to hermeneutics and eventually back to hermeneutic again as I consider the contribution of Dr. Robert A. Bennett to our subject, "African Americans and Biblical Hermeneutics." Dr. Bennett deals with hermeneutic, hermeneutics (synonymous with exegesis) and what he calls modes of Biblical interpretation.

As early as 1970, if not earlier, Bob produced a paper entitled "Biblical Hermeneutics and the Black Preacher." In revised form, it was published in the ITC *Journal*, Volume 1, Number II, Spring-1974. In his introduction, as others have done elsewhere, he calls attention to the (former) centrality of the Holy Scripture within the Black Church which interpreted the Bible as a message of blessing rather than curse, and to Black preaching which used the Bible in a discriminating way, passing over historically conditioned parts and rejecting other passages. He then calls upon the Black Church to reaffirm for today the historic centrality within its preaching.

Having thus written, Father Bennett proceeds to introduce the reader to the historical critical approach to Biblical study (even as Mr. Mason does in his criticism of the method), stating that it seeks to let the word spoken in another time and place speak again within our own situation—just as the slave ancestors, through *the gift of God's spirit* (italics added) related the word to ancient Israel to their existential setting. Biblical criticism he asserts, is a tool for Black people rather than a trick as it had been employed by whites against Blacks. It can be employed to their benefits by Black preachers. With this positive appraisal of Biblical critics, under the caption of "Hermeneutical Method and the Black Preacher" Bob defines and describes historical and literary criticism, then sets forth the various aspects of literary analysis which he refers to as the so-called "steps in exegesis" (which for him is hermeneutics); steps that are four in number, namely: Text Criticism, Form Criticism, Literary Criticism, and Tradition and Redaction Criticism. Noting that the preacher and exegete are ultimately concerned with what the Biblical revelation means to us today, he brings in the word "hermeneutic" as the name of the discipline which bridges the gap between the then of Biblical times and the now of God's word to his people. While Biblical criticism seeks to uncover the literal meaning or plain sense of what the human Biblical writer intended to say, and this may be adequate in some instances, some passages require more than the literal sense, an additional spiritual or mystical meaning which carries the thrust of God's word to us today.

At this point Father Bennett brings in four most important modes or interpretive principles used for getting at the more than literal meaning within certain portions of the Bible: Allegory, Typology, Christology, and Sensus Plenior. Reminding the reader that the first Christians used these modes of interpretation to relate Old Testament themes and events to the New Testament, he informs that the Church down through the ages has used them to relate the message of Scripture to its own day, Moreover, he goes on to say:

> Much of contemporary theology and preaching finds relevance through the Christological and typological interpretation of given passages. Thus, the Black Theology of Major Jones and the preaching in the black community, using the Christological approach see the work of Christ in our midst as the key to interpreting and proclaiming the divine word. James Cone and others who relate Old Testament themes and events to the contemporary black scene, not only as parallels, but as revelation working itself out in on-going history can be said to use a typological interpretation.

With Father Bennett's contribution we have before us then some representative Black views of what constitutes or should constitute African American hermeneutic, hermeneutics, and hermeneutic. Despite what I reported about Mr. Mason's negative critique of historical-literary Biblical criticism, all except in the case of James Cone, appear to be in agreement. Emphasis has been placed on a Black hermeneutic that is inherent in the preaching of the Black fathers who although they did not exegete, technically speaking, did so through God's Spirit. Yet, Biblical criticism is a tool that should be employed today—hermeneutics. Beyond that employment of hermeneutics is the employment of modes, particularly Christological and typological—to follow Dr. Bennett.

To what I have tried to present objectively I have several reactions. First of all, by way of corrective rather than negative criticism, I should say that almost to a man the writers idealize and romanticize the content and style of the fathers who always in their preaching produced positive and upbuilding sermons. Henry modifies his picture by referring to the best preaching among the Fathers. But surely they were among a minority. And in the old days before the Civil War, I am afraid that among most Black preachers in the North at least, Phyllis Wheatley with her "Negroes Black as Cain" would have been more acceptable than David Walker with his informing white people that he has read his Bible too but could find no reference to Cain's having been Black, or to Blacks' being of the seed of Cain.

I cannot agree with Father Bennett when he attributes a so-called "curse of Ham" to those who as a trick used the historical critical method, as he does. No, this trick was played first by the ancient Jewish rabbis, borrowed by the Christian Fathers such as Jerome, and brought over into the modern period.

These negative observations aside, I am greatly benefited. As one who cut his teeth on Biblical literalism (dare I say also Fundamentalism), fled to radical historical-literary criticism as described by Mr. Mason, for relief, then forced into a post radical historical-literary position, I have been blessed. Father Bennett especially has given me the identification of the principles, or should I say modes of interpretation used by even the uneducated Black Fathers and their worthy descendants. As I have heard Black Scholar after scholar extol the preaching of the Black Fathers, I have often said to myself, "Why doesn't someone analyze that preaching in order to see what their principles were? Now the answer has been given. Or has it? Permit me for the time being to let that question remain suspended in mid air, while I move ahead to say some more complimentary things.

Second, Father Bennett, in particular, has helped me move beyond a chastened historical-literary criticism that admits of the necessity and validity of using the so-called modes or principles of interpretation—the Christological and typological, to say nothing of the allegorical long outmoded. I have had difficulty with employing these modes, so it seems, even though I had at least intellectually formulated some principles of my own that admitted of that kind of "theological," spiritual interpretation, namely: Interpret the Bible in the light of all its contexts, historical, literary, geographical, cultural, etc,; interpret the Old Testament, yet also the New, in the light of God's revelation in Jesus Christ, and in the light of His continuing revelation through the Holy Spirit, even while permitting the Old Testament to retain its integrity. Undoubtedly, somewhere along the way, I was influenced by the "Guiding Principles for the Interpretation of the Bible" as accepted by the Ecumenical Study Conference held at Wadham College, Oxford, from June 29 to July 5, 1949—principles that I note are still recommended in books on Biblical Preaching:

1) The determination of the text;
2) the literary form of the passage;
3) the historical situation, the *sitz im leben*;

4) the meaning which the words had for the original
author and hearer or reader;

5) the understanding of the passage in the light of its total
context and the background out of which it emerged.

The heart of my problem has been, or so it seems, with
Bob's modes of interpretation. Intellectually, I could not afford
to employ them, while emotionally, in view of my own
principles, I was using them all along, ignorant or unaware of
what I was doing. Presently, almost, I have been persuaded to
accept intellectually, so that I more than just believe where I
cannot prove, embracing solely by faith. Even so, it seems that I
still hear myself praying, "Lord, I believe, help Thou my
unbelief."

Now finally, back to our question that we left dangling.
Given that the "new hermeneutic" is nothing more than the
old-time Black hermeneutic, that Black Biblical hermeneutics is
to employ the same steps as that of any other color, and that
everyone is to use the modes of interpretation, where does Black
Hermeneutics differ from any other?[1]

---

1. 7/9/87. Since doing this original rough draft, I have come into possession of J. Deotis
Roberts' volume *Black Theology Today*, which has a section on the subject.

Chapter 6

Biblical Characters, Events, Places and Images Remembered and Celebrated in Black Worship

The title of this article is a restatement and reduction of a much larger topic, "African and Biblical Bases for Black Worship and the Ways in which Biblical Events, Characters, Places and Images Parallel and Interweave Black Experience, and are Remembered and Celebrated in Worship," an extended project upon which I am constantly at work. It is to be noted, here, that I shall deal in this paper only with *Biblical* (i.e., not with African) characters, events, places, and images.

At the very beginning, I must say that what is here presented is to be viewed and evaluated as the first draft of a report of an investigation into the subject. The subject is so vast that several persons, working over an extended period of time, might give attention to it. Therefore, the best that I might hope for is that what is presented may serve as a suggestion for further research and writing.

Worship consists of several elements. This investigation was limited to songs, sermons, and prayers. In the course of the investigation I perused five hundred and fifty Spirituals, chiefly by title; two hundred and fifty Gospel Songs which date mainly from the 1930's to the present; fifty "Tindley" and similar Black Gospel Hymns which date from 1885 to 1935; and three hundred sermons which date from 1800 to the present. Roughly twenty-five prayers, dating from 1785 to the present, were reviewed.

BIBLICAL CHARACTERS AND EVENTS

Biblical characters and events may best be dealt with together, inasmuch as they are intimately related.

My research disclosed that some authorities have already produced works on characters and events as they have to do with songs, especially the Spirituals.

In his book, *Negro Folk Music, U.S.A.*, Harold Courlander notes that if Black religious songs are arranged in a somewhat chronological order they are equivalent to an oral version of the Bible. He proceeds to demonstrate by citing Spirituals that deal in historical succession (but not always in correct sequence) with Adam and Eve in the Garden of Eden, Noah and the flood, Moses, Joshua, David, Samson, Elijah, Job, Daniel, Judas, Jonah, Pilate's wife, John the Revelator, Gabriel, Judgment Day, the story of Jesus's birth and ministry, John the Baptist, and more.[1]

Various writers call attention to the fact that in the Spirituals one may find characters and events from different periods in biblical history mixed together. Moreover, in a single Spiritual one may find characters and events that span the whole course of Biblical history, from creation to the last judgment portrayed in the book of Revelation. Thus, Courlander gives special attention to a Spiritual usually known as "Job, Job" which alludes to significant scenes scattered throughout the Old and New Testaments, without any rigid sequence. He describes the version which he reproduces as follows:

> In the version given here, the song begins with Job in the first section; goes on in the second to tell about Judas, Pilate, and Pilate's wife; moves back to Joshua and the stopping of the sun in the third; follows in the fourth with scenes from the Revelation of St. John; continues with references to Gabriel in the fifth section; and in the book of Daniel. The choruses between stanzas vary, no two being exactly alike. They deal with Mt. Zion, the

---

1. Harold Courlander, *Negro Folk Music, U.S.A.* (New York: Columbia University Press, 1963), pp. 36-43.

Salvation train, Judgement Day, Elijah's chariot, and, finally, the resurrection.... [2]

With specific references to Spirituals, John Lovell, Jr. comments: "It is highly significant that with all the Biblical characters, incidents, parables, sermons, and historical features to choose from, the slave, in thousands of songs, selected relatively a few and turned these to only a few ends."[3] He follows up with a chart that presents what he calls "Use of Biblical Items in the Spiritual." In this chart he sets forth Biblical "people" and events in both Testaments. His list of characters for the Old Testament is as follows: Adam and Eve, Methusaleh, Noah, Abraham, Isaac, Jacob, Joseph, Moses, Pharaoh, Pharaoh's daughter, Joshua, Gideon, Samson, Delilah, Samuel, David, Ezekiel, Daniel, the Hebrew Children (Shadrach, Meshach, and Abednego), Nebuchadnezzar, and Jonah.

For the New Testament he lists: Jesus, Mary the Mother of Christ, John the Baptist, Apostle Peter, Apostle John, Apostle Thomas, Nicodemus, Mary and Martha, Lazarus, Dives, Pilate, Paul, and the Prodigal Son.

As important New Testament events, Lovell lists only the Birth of Christ, the Crucifixion of Christ, and the Resurrection of Christ. Commenting upon the lists, which are based upon five hundred Spirituals from a total of more than six thousand, he says:

A close comparison with the real people and happenings of the Bible will reveal the slave poet's broad or delicate emphases and variations, his outright departures, and something very important, the Biblical items, events, and people he does not emphasize. Note, for example, that Paul's reputation rests on his ability to pray rather than on his great apostleship; Joseph's great rulership is ignored; and Ruth, Esther, Solomon, Isaiah, Jeremiah, and Amos do not appear in the current list (although it is hard to say flatly that they are never mentioned in the songs).[4]

---

2. Ibid., p. 52.

3. John Lovell, Jr., *Black Song: The Forge and The Flame* (New York: The MacMillan Company, 1972), p. 257.

4. Ibid., pp. 258-262.

Still other lists of characters by different scholars are given by Lovell, each scholar giving his particular choices. In the opinion of the present writer, the following characters and events, according to number, are the outstanding ones: Eschatalogical Events (at the end of time, Day of Judgment, etc.), 68; Jesus' Ministry, 45; Jesus' Passion (sufferings), 17; Jesus's Birth, 11; Jesus' Triumph at the end of time, 7; Jesus' Resurrection, 5; Moses and the Exodus Event, 5; The Jacob Story, 5; Mary and Martha, 5; Joshua and Jericho, 3; Peter on the Water, and Healing Beggar, 3; Nicodemus, 3; Daniel, 2; Lazarus, the Beggar, 2; Elijah and the Chariot, 2; Paul and Silas in Jail, 2; Jeremiah, 1.

Of special significance are the eschatalogical events. These are drawn from scenes of the Last Judgment and apocalyptic passages in the Gospels, New Testament epistles, such as I Thessalonians and I Peter, and especially from the book of Revelation. Hardly a scene in Revelation is omitted from the Spirituals viewed as a whole, and the singers participate in the scenes by way of anticipation. Scenes in Revelation include: The Giving of a New Name; The Four and Twenty Elders; The Sounding of the Trumpet; The Fall of Babylon; The Great Gittin' Up Morning; Jesus Riding as a Conquering Warrior; The Raining Down of Fire; The Marching In of The Saints; The Casting Down of Crowns before the Lamb; The Crowning of Christ as Lord of All; The Gathering of the Number that No Man Can Number; The Singing of the Song of Moses and The Lamb; and the Coming Down of the New Jerusalem from Heaven.

It should be noted that the number which indicates frequency of titles of the five hundred Spirituals indexed by Lovell may be misleading. The number 5 with Moses does not show that the one Spiritual, "Go Down Moses," is cited thirty times in Lovell's text, and is the most common of all the Spirituals. Again, the number 1 by Jeremiah refers to the Spiritual "Balm in Gilead" which appears eight times in the text.

In the "Tindley" and kindred Gospel Hymns, there are relatively few references to Biblical characters and events. What references that appear deal chiefly with Jesus: three instances of his teaching; two with his trial before Pilate; two with his death on the cross; and one each with his walking on water, his last supper, his prayer in Gethsemane, and his giving the Great Commission. Other characters, each of whom is referred to only once, are: Daniel and his deliverance; Elisha, and Namaan who bathed in the Jordan; Mary, who sat at Jesus' feet; Lazarus, who begged at Dives' table; the repentant thief on the cross; Pilate; and Paul and Silas in prison.

References to characters predominate over events in the Gospel Songs. As might be suspected, the characters correspond primarily with those in the Spirituals. However, importance ratings may be different; and additional characters and events may appear. The chief character is Jesus, with ninety-eight of the two hundred fifty songs dealing with him. God, the Father, ranks second, with twenty having Him as their subject. Among other favorite characters, Daniel appears at the top of the list. Proportionately, twice as many of the Gospel Songs, in comparison with the Spirituals, deal with the crucifixion and death, resurrection, and final triumph of Jesus. The second coming of Jesus is the concern of fourteen of the Gospel Songs.

Instances of the addition of new characters appear in the examples that follow. To be noted as additions are Rebecca, Isaiah, Solomon, Mark, Luke, and Timothy. As raised in rank is Daniel; and Daniel, Paul and Silas appear frequently.

> I thought when I entered that city,
> My loved ones knew me well,
> They showed me all thro' heaven,
> The scenes are too num'rous to tell.
> I saw Abraham, Isaac, and Jacob,
> Mark, Luke, and Timothy;
> But I said, 'Let me bow down and worship
> The One who died for me.'[5]

> He walked into the furnace door
> with Shadrach, Meshach, Abednego.
> He took the heat out of the flame
> I know today, I know today, He's jus' the same.

> He was Daniel's stone arolling
> and Ezekiel's wheel aturning
> He was Moses's bush aburning,
> Solomon's Rose of Sharon,
> He was Jeremiah's mighty battle ax.[6]

---

5. *The New National Baptist Hymnal* (Nashville: National Baptist Publishing Board, 1977).

6. *Songs of Zion* (Nashville: Abingdon, 1981), Song #193.

I'm gonna live on forever,
Yes, I'm gonna live on forever,
Yes, I'm gonna live up in glory after awhile.
I'm going out sightseeing in Beulah,
March all around God's altar,
Walk and never tire,
Fly, Lord, and never falter.
Move on up a little higher,
Meet old man Daniel.
Move on up a little higher,
Meet the Hebrew children.
Move on up a little higher,
Meet Paul and Silas.
Move on up a little higher,
Meet my friends and kindred.
Move on up a little higher,
Meet my loving mother.
Move on up a little higher,
Meet that Lily of the Valley,
Feast with the Rose of Sharon.[7]

Well Isaiah said he saw him
    with his dyed garments on,
coming from the land of Bozrah,
    treading the wine press alone.

Daniel said he saw him as a chief
    cornerstone,
I'm gonna wait right here for my
    Jesus till he comes.

Rebecca said she saw him while
    kneeling down in prayer,
He came down through the elements
    and his glory filled the air,
With a rainbow on his shoulder
    and the government in his hand,
I'm gonna wait right here on my
    Jesus till he comes.[8]

----

7. Langston Hughes & Arna Bontemps, eds., *The Book of Negro Folklore* (New York: Mead & Company, Inc., 1983), p. 324.

8. Anthony Heilbut, *The Gospel Sound*, Updated and Revised (New York: Limelight Editions, 1985), p.78.

As James Weldon Johnson states in the preface to *God's Trombones*, first published in 1927, "there was a stereotyped sermon which had no definite subject, and which was quite generally preached; it began with the creation, went on to the fall of man, rambled through the trials and tribulations of the Hebrew children, came down to the redemption by Christ, and ended with the Judgment Day."[9]

In similar fashion, some Black preachers today, no matter what their text or subject, may include in a single sermon references to nearly all the characters and events in the Bible—from Genesis through Revelation.

The chart which follows presents in chronological order the Old Testament characters dealt with in the sermons, the number of sermons upon them, and the events associated with them:

Character	Sermons	Events
Adam and Eve	2	Their fall in the Garden
Job (as a patriarch)	2	His suffering and faith
Abraham	2	His exercise of faith, (often used as example) and near offering of Isaac
Isaac	2	His cleaning of wells and near sacrifice
Jacob	3	Story of his flight from and return to Canaan
Rachel	1	Her death
Joseph	5	Whole story of, and his teaching on Providence
Moses	21	Whole story from call, through Exodus, and viewing of Promised Land
Pharaoh	2	His defeat at Red Sea
Joshua	2	God's command for him to "go on," and his order to go into the "wood country"
Caleb	1	His asking for a mountain
Deborah	2	Her being a mother in Israel
Gideon	1	His conquering with a small band

---

9. James Weldon Johnson, *God's Trombones: Seven Negro Sermons In Verse* (New York: The Viking Press, 1927), pp. 1-2.

David & Goliath.........2	David's defeat of Goliath (but with twenty sermons based upon the book of Psalms, presumably as written by David).	
Elijah.....................3	His victory on Mt. Carmel (often cited as example)	
Elisha.....................2	His ministry with Namaan	
Namaan...................1	His bathing in Jordan River	
Jonah.....................1	His having been given a "second chance"	
Amos.....................1	As being a prophet	
Isaiah.....................1	His call—but with ten sermons based upon book of Isaiah	
Hezekiah..................1	His prayer in distress	
Jeremiah..................3	Conversations with God (but with several references to "Balm in Gilead")	
Habbakkuk.................1	His exercise of "Watchtower Faith"	
Ezekiel....................0	But with four sermons on "Dry Bones"	
Daniel, (Nebuchadnezzar.3 and Hebrew Children)	Deliverance and Faithfulness	
Malachi...................1	His appeal to tithing	
Haggai.....................1	His appeal to rebuild Temple	
Nehemiah 1	His rebuilding of walls of Jerusalem	
Esther.....................1	Her being God's Woman	

With respect to the New Testament, seventy of the sermons, apart from those on the parables, deal with aspects of Jesus' life and ministry. The events and number of sermons are as follows: Birth, 6; Temptation, 5; In Synagogue at Nazareth, 3; Entry into Jerusalem, 3; Upper Room and Last Supper, 6; Trial, 1; Crucifixion, 2; Resurrection, 4; Giving of Great Commission, 3; Final Triumph, 13.

Fourteen of the sermons deal with parables told by Jesus, and his other teachings. Among the parables, often viewed as actual happenings, the number of sermons on each are: The Good Samaritan, 6; The Prodigal Son, 2; Dives and Lazarus, 2; The Unjust Steward, 1; The Friend Knocking at Midnight, 1; The Rich Fool, 1; The Lost Sheep, 1; and the Lost Coin, 1.

Other sermons, having to do with Jesus' miracles, are based upon: Feeding of Multitude, 3; Healing the man at the Pool, 2; Healing of Boy with Demon, 2; Healing of "Legion," 3; Giving Sight to Bartimaeus, 1; Healing of Woman with Issue of Blood, 1; and the Raising of Lazarus, 1.

In addition to Jesus, New Testament characters treated are: John the Baptist, preaching and baptizing in the wilderness, 2; Peter, and incidents related to him as a disciple, 5; Peter and John healing the beggar, 2; the three Marys at the tomb, 3; Martha, and her conversation with Jesus about Lazarus, 1; Paul, 1, but with fifty of the sermons based upon his epistles; and John the Revelator, 6.

Harold A. Carter, in his book, *The Prayer Tradition of Black People*, quotes a statement of John Lovell, Jr. to the effect that prayer is another literary form in which the Spiritual specializes, citing several.[10] The same comment may be made about the "Tindley" songs and the Gospel Songs, numerous examples of which could be given. And although Carter gives what he regards as a prayer that is typical in style and content, that prayer refers to no Biblical character or event. Of the fifteen prayers and excerpts from prayers presented in Carter's book, only four do contain references. The first of these refers to Elijah praying at a mountain, apparently Sinai; the second, to Daniel in the lion's den and the Hebrew children in the furnace; the third, to Job; and the fourth to Jesus' statement to Peter about the church and the gates of hell, and to Samson's setting the Philistine wheat fields afire.[11]

Four other prayers, dating from 1785 to the present, contain references, but two of these are reconstructed by the Black writers James Baldwin[12] and Richard Wright. Two of the four prayers refer to Daniel and the Hebrew children only. Richard Wright's prayer contains references to Israel's Exodus out of Egypt, Dry Bones, the Hebrew children, the sun's standing

---

10. Harold A. Carter, *The Prayer Tradition of Black People* (Valley Forge: Judson Press, 1976), p.95.

11. Ibid., pp. 36-91.

12. James Baldwin, *Go Tell It On The Mountain* (New York: The New American Library of World Literature, Inc., A Signet Book, 1954), p.59.

still at Gibeon, the fall of the walls of Jericho, Jonah and the whale, Jesus' walking on water, Jesus' being raised from the dead, Jacob, and Saul—all with God's having done something. The fourth prayer, prayed by an old lady shortly after the Civil War, refers to Daniel and the Hebrew children, to "sinking" Peter, and to "weeping" Mary.[13]

Interestingly, the Angel Gabriel, so popular in Black culture, does not appear in relation to events with which he is associated!

BIBLICAL PLACES

Despite the fact that much should be said introductorily about Biblical places, I proceed directly to deal with them by way of tabulation.

In two hundred and seventeen of the Spirituals, eight places stand out. The names and number of references to them, in descending order, are: New Jerusalem, 68; Places in Jesus' ministry, 48; Heaven, 46; Jordan River, 24; Egypt, 19 directly, but numerous times indirectly; the seven churches to which John wrote, 8; Promised Land, 4; Patmos, 1.

Although ninety percent of the "Tindley" and similar songs are oriented toward heaven, seven of them refer to an equal number of places, according to number, as follows: Heaven, 6; Jordan River, 2; Calvary, 2; Red Sea, Wilderness, Sea of Galilee, and New Jerusalem, one each.

Eleven places, apart from the list in the song which follows, appear as the choices in the Gospel Songs. Names with number of references are: Heaven, 25, one tenth of all; Calvary, 8; Jordan River, 4; Beulah Land, 4; Zion, 3; Canaanland and New Jerusalem, 2 each; Bethany, Galilee, Promised Land, and Bethlehem, 1 each.

Winning the prize for the largest number of places in a single song is "City Called Jerusalem" which contains the following stanza:

> There are many important cities
>   where the great Apostles went,
> Rome, Athens, Thessalonica, Antioch and Corinth.

---

13. Ellen Wright and Michel Fabre, eds., *Richard Wright Reader* (New York: Harper & Row, 1978), pp. 297-298.

The John in Revelation when called to come
  up higher,
Wrote to Ephesus and Smyrna, Pergamos
  and Thyatira;
Sardis, Philadelphia, Laodicea—a letter
  around,
But none was like the city John saw
  coming down.[14]

Places referred to in or related to the sermons, many on the basis of Paul's letters, number forty-nine. According to name and number of references they are: Jerusalem, 28; Palestine, 12; Rome, 9; Babylon, in the Old Testament where it is an actual city, and in Revelation where it is a symbol of Rome, 8; Galatia, on the basis of Paul's letter, 7; Galilee, 6; Jordan River, 6; Jericho, 5; Egypt, 5; Philippi, on the basis of Paul's letter, 4; Wilderness near Jordan River, 3; Sinai Wilderness, 3; Bethlehem, New Jerusalem, Red Sea, Nazareth, Calvary, Ephesus (Paul's letter), and Patmos, 3 each; Sea of Galilee, Gadara, whole World, Ethiopia, Mt. Moriah, Heaven, and Gethsemane, 2 each; and once each for Bethany, Bethel, Beulah Land, Canaan, Colossae, Damascus, Dead Sea, Ebenezer, Golgotha, Israel, Jabbok, Macedonia, Mar's Hill, Mediterranean Sea, Mt. Ararat, Mt. Carmel, Mt. Sinai, Mount of Temptation, Ninevah, Persia, Samaria, Spain, and Syria.

Only four places are named in the prayers: an unspecified mountain, obviously Sinai; the jail in which Paul and Silas were placed; the fiery furnace, and Calvary.

In the lists of places remembered and celebrated in songs, sermons, and prayers, some ten places stand out prominently. It should be noted, however, that Biblical places play a very important part otherwise in Black worship: in the naming of churches, names range from Antioch to Zion, and are of places located primarily in Palestine, Syria, Asia Minor, Macedonia, and Greece.

Frequently actual places are allegorized or spiritualized as in the instances of Canaan, Promised Land, Egypt, Wilderness, and Jordan River. Some places may be symbolic or figurative locations, such as New Jerusalem, Beulah Land and even Heaven.

---

14. Anthony Heilbut, *The Gospel Sound*, p. 102

By way of contrast, it is interesting to note that Black Americans did not give to towns and settlements which they populated and governed Biblical names as white Americans so often did. Of some sixty-seven such towns and settlements, according to records in 1937-38, only three bore such names: Nicodemus, Illinois; Mt. Carmel, Mississippi; and Mizpah, New Jersey.[15]

Using Baltimore, Maryland, as an example, Olin P. Moyd notes that twice as many Black Baptist churches take their names from Biblical mountains as from Biblical saints. He attributes theological significance to the use of mountains for names, and cites Mount Sinai, Mount Carmel, Mount of Olives, and Mount Zion, as representative.[16]

BIBLICAL IMAGES

By its very nature as an Oriental book, and as a book that treats of spiritual matters, the Bible is filled with images, symbols and figures of speech. God, being Spirit, can only be spoken of in figurative language. So it is also with respect to other entities in relation to God. The people Israel and the Church, the New Israel, are spoken of as sheep, sons or children of God, wife, and bride to name a few metaphors. Moreover, some entities such as death and heaven are treated symbolically. Still again, as noted under the discussion of *places*, some actual places such as Egypt, Canaan, Wilderness, Promised Land, Jordan River are allegorized or spiritualized in worship.

In this paper the treatment of images is limited basically to *metaphors* that are applied to God and to Jesus Christ. The ones presented appear chiefly in poetic sections of the Old Testament, especially in psalms both in and outside the book of Psalms, and in the poetic sections of the prophetical books, plus others that appear in the New Testament with reference to Jesus Christ.

A catalog of some images of God in the Old Testament includes the following: Alpha and Omega, Ancient of Days, Creator, Cup, Deliverer, Dwelling Place, Father, Fire (consuming), Fortress, Help, Helper, Helper of the Fatherless,

---

15. Merl R. Eppse, *The Negro, Too, in American History* (Nashville: National Publication Company, 1943), pp. 540-541.

16. Olin P. Moyd, *Redemption in Black Theology* (Valley Forge: Judson Press, 1979), p. 194.

Holy One, Holy One of Israel, Husband, Judge, Keeper, King, King of Glory, Light, Lord of Hosts, Most High, Most High God, Portion (chosen), Rearguard, Redeemer, Refuge, Refuge In Day of Trouble, Rock, Rock of Refuge, Rock of Salvation, Salvation, Shade, Shade on Right Hand, Shepherd, Shield, Stay, Strength, Stronghold, Stronghold for the Oppressed, Sun, Tower (strong), and Upholder of My Life.

Images of Jesus in the New Testament include those in the Messianic passages in the Old Testament which appear especially in the book of Isaiah, such as: Immanuel, Wonderful Counselor, Mighty God, Everlasting Father, Prince of Peace, and the Servant. To himself Jesus applied the figures of Bread, Door, Light, Resurrection, Life, Shepherd, Vine, Way, Truth.

In the Gospels, Epistles and Revelation images applied to Jesus by the first Christians include the following: Adam, Amen, Anointed, Cornerstone, Firstborn of the Dead, Guardian, Head, Image, King, King of Jews, King of Kings, Lamb, Lamb of God, Paschal Lamb, Lamp, Leader, Lily of the Valley, Lion of Tribe of Judah, Lord, Lord of Lords, Master, Name, Passover, Physician, Pioneer, and Perfecter, Priest, Rabbi, Righteousness, Rock, Root of David, Rose of Sharon, Ruler of the Kings of Earth, Savior, Shepherd, Son of God, Son of Man, Son of David, Star, Stone, Sun, Water, Wisdom, Witness, and Word.

"God," in the Spirituals indexed by Lovell, appears as subject twenty times. The pronoun "He" is used four times. God is addressed as "Lord" eight times, and He is called a Man of War once. "Jesus" as subject is used thirty-two times; and he is referred to otherwise in the following terms: Lord, 62 times; King, 9; Lamb, 4; Savior, 3; "He," 3; Door, 2; Prince of Peace, 2; Rock, 2; Vine, Man of Calvary, and Bread, once each.

In the "Tindley" and kindred Gospel Hymns, God is addressed as Father, and God most High, and is referred to as the Rock of Ages. Jesus is addressed as King seven times, as Savior seven times, and is called Lamb, Lily of the Valley, Son of God, Truth Divine, and Word of Life, once each.

Most of the images in the Gospel Songs are applied to Jesus. God is addressed simply as God or Father, and is referred to under several images in a single song, such as in the instance that follows:

Black Worship 91

He's worthy! God's worthy! Almighty Creator!
Alpha, Omega, Beginning and the End!
Holy, holy Lord God Almighty
Which was and is and is to come.
Blessing and glory, wisdom and power,
God of my Rock, In Him will I trust!
My Strong Tower and my Refuge
Savior, Deliverer and soon-coming King.[17]

God is, further, called Rock, Sword, and Shield.

In a sampling of the Gospel Songs favorite images for Jesus are: Bread of Heaven; Cornerstone; Fortress; King; King of Kings; Lamb; Lily of the Valley; Lion of Judah; Lord of All; Master; Rock of Ages; Solid Rock; Rose of Sharon; Savior; Shepherd; Shield; Son of God; Bright Morning Star; Sword; Way; Wonderful.

Biblical images that refer to Jesus in the sermons, thirty-five plus those in Isaiah, chapter 9, are, in alphabetical order: All Sufficient One; Alpha and Omega; Author and Perfecter; The Christ; King; Heavenly King; King of Kings; King of Zion: Lamb; Light; Lily of the Valley; Lion of Judah; Logos; Lord; Lord Jesus; Lord of Life; Lord of Lords; Passover; Priest; Prince of Peace; Redeemer; Resurrection and Life; Rock in a Weary Land; Rose of Sharon; Savior; Shelter in a Time of Storm; Shepherd; Son of God; Star; Stay; Suffering Servant; Vine; Word; and Wonderful.

Especially in the Gospel Songs and sermons, images based upon modern experiences are employed to augment those found in the Bible. Indicative of some used in a sermon are Bread in a Starving Land, Water in Dry Places, Integrative Personality, Cosmic Mind, Unique Idea, and Liberator—for Jesus; and for God: All-Powerful and Knowing, Merciful; Patient Ultimate Reality; Ground of Being; All-Sufficient One; Enabler; Provider; Sustainer; and Righteous-Victorious One.[18]

Images in the prayers consist of Rock in a Weary Land, Shelter in a Storm, Holy Father, Father Almighty, Lamp, and Light, for God. For Jesus they are King, Master, Lamb, and Redeemer.

---

17. *New Inspirational Soul* (Newbury Park, Ca.: Lexicon Music, Inc., 1984), p.3.

18. Joseph A. Johnson, Jr., *The Soul of the Black Preacher* (Philadelphia: United Church Press, 1971), pp. 164-165.

CONCLUSION

At the beginning of this paper it was stated that the subject is so vast that several persons, working over an extended period of time, might give attention to it. Such an assertion receives support in noting that only five hundred fifty Spirituals of a total of more that six thousand that are extant were dealt with, and that chiefly by title. Further, and still with reference only to songs, standard hymns, such as those by Watts and the Wesleys, tabernacle and revival hymns, etc., were not considered; yet these abound with references to Biblical characters, events, places and images. Further still, there remain to be investigated those elements of worship additional to songs, sermons and prayers such as testimonies, Scripture readings, responsive readings, calls to worship, and so on.

Indeed, "the fields are ripe unto harvest," and the prospects are abundant.

Chapter 7

Three Thousand Years of Biblical Interpretation with Reference to Black Peoples

In the land of Palestine, known also from antiquity as the Holy Land, stand two mountains, which are not far apart and which face each other. In between lies a valley. By the ancient Hebrews, one mountain, called Gerizim, was referred to as the "Mount of Blessing." The other, called Ebal, was referred to as the "Mount of Cursing." Using a figure of speech, with reference to the Bible, we may compare the Bible to the valley between the two mountains, and ask a question: "To which of these mountains does the Bible—or rather, interpretations of the Bible,—belong?" To the "Mount of Blessing" or the "Mount of Cursing?"

Granted that the Bible, along with interpretations of it, have proved to be and continue to be sources of blessings to millions of people. It is also true that these have been and continue to be sources of some of the greatest curses humankind has known. Upon the basis of the Bible and interpretations of it Orthodox Jew has killed Orthodox Jew; Orthodox Jew has killed Christian Jew; Gentile has murdered Jew; Christian has murdered Christian. In no instance, however, have the Bible and interpretations of it led to such murder, whether physical, psychological, social, or spiritual, as in the case of Black peoples. As will be noted, such murder goes back to ancient times, and is still being committed today.

This lecture has as its purpose to review the history of the Bible and its interpretation with reference to Black peoples, from the very beginnings of the Bible itself, as collections of literature at various times, to the Bible as it exists today primarily in English translation, and as it is still interpreted today. Hence the title of the lecture is "Three Thousand Years of Biblical Interpretation with Reference to Black Peoples."

Foundational for a treatment of the subject is knowledge of the history of the Bible and its canonization: knowledge of the fact that, according to critical historical-literary study, what now constitutes the Bible came into existence, in stages, across more than twelve hundred years; and that canonization consisted of a series of processes that occurred, say, roughly from 600 B.C. to A.D. 400. Following the collection of literature into what may be referred to as the sacred Scriptures at any given stage along the way, and canonization at any given stage, came translation of the Hebrew scriptures, first into Greek; then creation of Christian New Testament writings in Greek; followed by translation into Latin, English and other such languages as now exist.

Once there was a Bible, at whatever stage at a given time, interpretation began. Thus there appears in what is now the Bible *inner* or *intra* Biblical interpretation.[1] This type of interpretation was succeeded by interpretation of the complete Bible, first of the Hebrew Scriptures plus Christian writings regarded as Scripture.

Interpretation as a process, begun within the Bible itself, continued and continues in all literature related to the Bible, that is, extra-Biblical literature, which must include translations of originals inasmuch as all translation is by its very nature also interpretation.

Bodies of extra-Biblical literature, arranged in a more or less chronological order, include the following: the translation of the Hebrew Scriptures into Greek, the Septuagint (250-100 B.C.); the Apocrypha and Pseudepigrapha of the Old Testament (150 B.C.—A.D. 150); the Qumran Writings (150 B.C.—A.D. 150); the writings of Philo and Josephus (25 B.C.—A.D. 100); the New Testament books (A.D. 50-100); early rabbinical interpretations such as are found in the early Midrashim, Haggadah, and the Palestinian and Babylonian Talmuds, plus Targums (A.D. 200-600); New Testament Apocryphal and

----

1. For a discussion of *inner* or *intra* Biblical interpretaiton, one may consult James L. Kugel and Rowan A. Greer, *Early Biblical Interpretation* (Philadelphia: The Westminster Press, 1986).

Pseudepigraphal writings (primarily of the second and third centuries A.D.); Targums (A.D. 200, and later); Islamic Literature (A.D. 625 and later); Jewish and Christian interpretations of the Middle Ages (A.D.600-1400); and for our purposes, primarily Christian interpretations of modern times, including interpretations by Black peoples (1400-1987).

Discussion of so vast a body of literatures must of necessities be limited to a very broad outline at best. With respect to filling in the outline, all that the lecturer can hope for is akin to that hope expressed by a Black Biblical scholar of nearly a hundred years ago. Bishop Benjamin T. Tanner, in the Dedication of his monograph, *The Color of Solomon—What?*:

> To the rising scholars of the colored race, the writer dedicates the monograph with the hope that the subject which it discusses, and others akin to it, will receive such treatment at their hands as will vindicate the colored races of the earth and save them from the delusion: "The leading race in all history has been the white race."[2]

The Biblical Text and Intra-Biblical Interpretation

Preliminary to a consideration of interpretation within the Bible, with reference to Black peoples, must come a prior consideration of the presence of Black peoples, or of peoples, whom the Biblical writers regarded as Black, in the Biblical text itself. Such a presence is determinable by the use of words or terms employed to designate *black* when applied to persons and peoples—Hebrew, Greek, and Latin. Relevant words and terms are *Shahar*, in Hebrew, meaning black, and used twice denoting skin or complexion, apart from occurrences associated with color caused by disease; *Hum*, in Hebrew of doubtful meaning, and limited to Genesis, chapter 30;[3] *Kedar*, in Hebrew, meaning black, and occurring some twelve times; *Cush*, and related words such as Cushite, in Hebrew, which occurs some fifty times, and bearing a color notion through most typical visual features;

---

2. Benjamin Tucker Tanner, *The Color of Solomon—What?* (Philadelphia: African Methodist Episcopal Book Concern, 1895).

3. See Athalya Brenner, *Colour Terms In the Old Testament*, Journal For The Study of The Old Testament, Supplement Series, no. 21 (Sheffield, England: Department of Biblical Studies, The University of Sheffield, 1982), 57, 63, 95.

Hoshek, in Hebrew, which refers to darkness; *Ethiopia, melas, niger*, and related terms in Greek; and *Ethiopia* and *Niger* in Latin—all of which have to do with black color.

The Greek and Latin terms are used to translate the Hebrew word Cush and related terms in the Old Testament; the Latin term *niger* is used to translate the corresponding word in the New Testament. In treating the identification of Black persons and peoples, the use of words is limited to include primarily *Cush* and related terms in the Old Testament (disregarding Kedar, Ham, and even Phinehas, which for now over a hundred years has been stated to mean "the Negro"); and Ethiopia and Niger in the New Testament.

Of some fifty occurrences of the word Cush and related terms in the Old Testament, half refer to individual persons or peoples. In the main, the references are factual statements. Of these the vast majority are judgments of God upon the Cushites (Ethiopians) similar to or identical with God's judgments upon other peoples, and without pejorative connotation based upon color. With such an opinion as the forestated, those of Black Biblical scholars are in agreement. Thus, in writing about the Biblical text with reference to color, Robert A. Bennett states, "Blacks in the Bible are mentioned favorably and become a symbol of God's love for all people."[4] Similarly, the Reverend Jacob A. Dyer in his booklet, *The Ethiopian in the Bible*, writes:

> I know of a certain author who has produced some excellent works. However, after reading a number of his books, I observed that his black and Jewish characters were never honorable. Whatever part they played, there was something about them that one could not admire. If his books were historical, it could be contended that he had recorded the facts as he found them; but as a literary composer, the characters he produced simply reflect his own attitude towards certain groups. Neither in the Old Testament nor in the New does the literature which constitutes the Bible reflect any such attitude towards non-whites or persons of black or dark complexion.[5]

---

4. Robert Avon Bennett, *God's Work of Liberation* (Wilton, Conn.: Morehouse Barlow Co., 1976), 78f.

5. Jacob A. Dyer, *The Ethiopian in The Bible* (New York: Vantage Press, 1974), 62.

An exception to the opinions just stated may or may not appear in the Song of Songs, Chapter 1:5, with reference to the appearance of the maiden: whether she is black *and* beautiful, or black *but* beautiful. Again, despite the opinions, there are at least two instances of texts within the Old Testament that reveal themselves as being cases of intra-Biblical interpretation. These are the explanatory glosses with reference to Ham's being the father of Canaan (Genesis 9:18, 22) and the explanatory comment at Numbers 12:1 with regard to Moses' having married a Cushite wife.

If, (as it appears now or will appear later), the word *Ham* did not mean *black* at the time the Noah story was written, and if the term *Hum* was not replaced by *Shahar* which is employed in the area of color terms only during the exilic and post-exilic periods, as argued by Athatlya Brenner in her book *Colour Terms in the Old Testament*, then Ham as the father of Canaan would mean nothing with regard to the color of the Canaanites.[6] This would come later, as will be seen, when we deal with interpretations of the rabbis, beginning in the second century A.D. where a different interpretation of the gloss "Ham the father of Canaan" is called for. And, to be sure, modern historical-literary scholars do have their interpretations, as did the scholars who preceded them, in deriving *ham* from *hamas* or a similar word and interpreting it to mean *black.*[7]

Two things may be said about the gloss at Numbers 12:1. It appears out of context, and the problem appears to be related to Aaron's and Miriam's status as prophets over against the status of Moses. Secondly, as has been observed by others, whatever the bone of contention among the siblings, God disapproved of the behavior of Aaron and Miriam and took sides with Moses.[8]

Interpretation in the Septuagint

From intra-Biblical interpretation, the next step is to interpretation of the Bible as it existed at the time of its first translation. The earliest translation of the original Biblical text is that of the Septuagint, from Hebrew-Aramaic into Greek. As has

---

6. Brenner, 57.

7. Ibid, 227. See also 58-64, notes 19, 20, 21, and 22.

8. For example, see Frank M. Snowden, Jr., *Blacks in Antiquity: Ethiopians In The Greco-Roman Experience* (Cambridge: Harvard Univerisity Press, Belnap Press, 1970), 202.

been stated, every translation is an interpretation. Necessary then is it to investigate how the translators dealt with the matter of black color. Two passages will suffice: Genesis 9:25, which has to do with the "curse of Canaan," and Songs of Songs 1:5, which has to do with the color of the maiden. With respect to the curse of Canaan, it has often been observed that one manuscript of the Septuagint has "cursed be *Ham.*" References to this one instance have been made by writers in modern times, some of whom argue that such a translation is proof that the original Hebrew text intended to place the curse on *Ham* rather than upon Canaan.[9] The latter assume, of course, that *Ham* in the original Hebrew meant *black.* What this one manuscript may show at best is a move in the so-called Intertestamental Period towards a "curse-on-Ham" position in some circles, or by a translator or scribe, even though *ham* may not necessarily at the time refer to blackness.

The conjunction in Song of Songs 1:5 may be translated as either *and* or *but*, in both Hebrew and Greek. Translated *and*, it is complimentary; translated *but*, it is pejorative. According to the intensive investigations of Frank M. Snowden, Jr., early commentators translated the conjunction *and*, as it appears in the Septuagint.[10]

Interpretation in the O.T. Apocrypha-Pseudepigrapha and Qumran Writings

A study of the Old Testament Apocryphal and Pseudepigraphal writings, and those of Qumran, reveals an absence of interpretations of the Biblical text with reference to Black peoples. All in all, there are thirteen references to Ethiopia or Ethiopians in the Apocrypha-Pseudepigrapha: six with reference to geographical locations; four with reference to historical events, without comment; two in the form of prophetic judgments; and one with reference to the Ethiopians as a stout-hearted people. Thus, there is one complimentary passage, but it does not refer to a text in the Bible.

---

9. For example, Jack P. Lewis, *A Study of the Interpretation of Noah And The Flood In Jewish And Christian Literature* (Leiden: E.J. Brill, 1968), 119, and Arthur C. Custance, *Noah's Three Sons* (Grand Rapids, Mich.: Zondervan Publishing House, 1975), 25.

10. Snowden, 198.

A prominent Biblical scholar investigated these books with an apparent purpose of detecting any that might refer to Negroes, especially. At first, he appears to have had a suspicion that one passage in Jubilees, called the "Little Genesis," might be relevant, but concluded that the passage in question, Chapter 10:29-34, which reveals the story of Noah's curse of Canaan does not connect the curse to the Negro race.[11] A question is inherent in his conclusion, however, for much depends upon the identity of Negroes in a given person's mind.

Upon the basis of a check of Biblical references in the Qumran literature, using the list of Scriptural references compiled by Theodore H. Gaster, there are no interpretations of pertinent Biblical texts referring to Black persons or peoples.[12]

Interpretation in Philo and Josephus

Once more, as in the instance of his study of the Old Testament Apocrypha and Pseudepigrapha, Jack P. Lewis asserts that neither Philo nor Josephus interprets the Old Testament passages here under consideration in a way derogatory of Black people.[13] Further, it may be observed, neither writer interprets "Ham" to mean *Black*. For them, the interpretation is "hot" or "heat." Philo's treatment of the Ham/Canaan story is allegorical.

In dealing with Ham's descendants, Josephus singles out Cush in his *Antiquities of the Jews* and writes: "time has not at all hurt the name of Cush; for the Ethiopians, over whom he reigned, are even at this day, both by themselves and by all men in Asia, called Cushites."[14]

In other parts of his *Antiquities*, which is a rewriting of the Old Testament history, Josephus recounts a story of Moses' marriage to an Ethiopian princess, an account that does not appear in the Bible, but will appear somewhat differently in later Jewish writings. Without interpretative comments he reproduces the account of the Cushite in II Samuel 18; that of the Queen of

----

11. Lewis, 31.

12. Theodore H. Gaster, *The Dead Sea Scriptures In English Translation* (Garden City, New York: Doubleday & Company, Anchor Books, 1956), 343ff.

13. Lewis, 73ff.; 179.

14. Flavius Josephus, *Antiquities of the Jews*, 6.2, trans. William Whiston in *The Works of Flavius Josephus* (Hartford, Conn.: S.S. Scranton Co., 1903), 40.

Sheba, whom he identifies as Queen of Egypt and Ethiopia; and those accounts of other Cushites—Zerah, Taharka, Ebed-Melech—in a matter of fact manner, without interpretative comment.[15]

Anticipating the rabbinical interpretations of the Noah story that will later appear in Genesis Rabbah of the Midrashim, and in the Babylonian Talmud, shortly after the time of Josephus, it might be well to give another excerpt from Josephus, one dealing with Noah's curse: "... but for Ham, he did not curse him, by reason of his nearness in blood, but cursed his posterity; and when the rest of them escaped that curse, God inflicted it on the children of Canaan."[16]

Interpretation in the New Testament

During the lifetime of Josephus, the books that comprise the New Testament were being written. Of the twenty-seven books that constitute the canon, only one, the book of Acts, Chapters 8:26-39 and 13:1, contains references to Black persons and peoples. Both passages are reports of matters of fact, without interpretative comment with respect to color.

Ancient Rabbinical Interpretation

Ancient rabbinical literature abounds with interpretations of the Old Testament both with respect to peoples and persons who are considered black in the Biblical text and those who are regarded as, or said to be black by the rabbis. The interpretations that concern us appear in the collection of midrashim known as Midrash Rabbah-Genesis, dated variously A.D.200-400, and the Babylonian Talmud, Tractate Sanhedrin, dated as early as A.D. 500, but as in the case of Midrash Rabbah-Genesis, containing material much older. Additionally there are Targums, dating from uncertain provenance but by some dated in final form from the fourth and fifth centuries A.D.[17]

---

15. Ibid, 225-308, passim.

16. Ibid, 41.

17. See Fred G. Bratton, *A History of The Bible* (Boston: Beacon Press, 1959), 236.

Apart from the Targums, classical locations of interpretations with reference to Black persons and peoples are Midrash Rabbah-Genesis XXXVI: 7-8; Babylonian Talmud, Sanhedrin 108b; and Midrash Rabbah-Genesis XXII:5-6. The first of these has a curse to fall on Ham, not directly but through Ham's fourth son, Canaan, who will be ugly and dark-skinned (the degree of color being dependent upon the translator of the original). The second asserts that Ham came forth from the Ark black, having been turned that color because, contrary to prohibitions he, along with the dog and the raven, had copulated while aboard the Ark. The third locus deals not with a curse nor mark upon Cain but with his rejected sacrifice (Genesis 4:5).

As translated, Midrash Rabbah-Genesis reads in part:

> R. Huna said in R. Joseph's name: (Noah declared), "you have prevented me from begetting a fourth son, therefore your seed will be ugly and dark-skinned." R. Hiyya said: "Ham and the dog copulated in the Ark, therefore Ham came forth black-skinned while the dog publicly exposes its copulation...[18]

It is to be noted that Graves and Patai, in their book *Hebrew Myths: The Book of Genesis*, relate the passage in Sanhedrein 108b to other sources such as *Tanhuma Noah* 13, 15, and produce the following additonal narrative:

> Moreover, because you twisted your head around to see my nakedness, your grandchildren's hair shall be twisted into kinks, and their eyes, red; again, because your lips jested at my misfortune, theirs shall swell; and because you neglected my nakedness, they shall go naked, and their male members shall be shamefully elongated. Men of this race are called Negroes.[19]

---

18. *Midrash Rabbah, Genesis*, eds. Rabbi Dr. H. Freedman and Maurice Simon, foreword by Rabbi Dr. Isidore Epstein (London: The Soncino Press, 1939), chap. xxxvi, 7-8, 293.

19. Robert Graves and Raphael Patai, *Hebrew Myths: The Book of Genesis* (New York: Greenwich House, 1983), 121. *Tanhuma Noah* 13f. is also cited in C.G. Montefiore and H. Loewe, eds. and trans., *A Rabbinic Anthology* (London; Macmillan & Co., Ltd., 1938; repr., New York: Shocken Books, 1974), 56.

Midrash Rabbah, Genesis XXII: 6 translated, reads:

And Cain was very wroth /wayyihar/ and his
countenance fell: [His face] became like a firebrand
[with the editorial note, Blackend].[20]

Upon these statements will hang later interpretations of
the Bible with reference to Black persons and peoples among
Jews, then Muslims, then Christians; and through them they will
be spread around the world as a deadly poison. Thereafter all the
children, not only of Canaan, but also of Ham, will be
considered to be black: Cushites (Ethiopians); Mitzraimites
(Egyptians); Phutites; and Canaanites.

Interpretation in New Testament Apocrypha and Pseudepigrapha

As in the case of the New Testament itself, so is there no
interpretation of Biblical texts with reference to Black persons
and peoples in the New Testament Apocrypha and
Pseudepigrapha.[21] However, it is to be noted that some of these
writings, dated as early as the second and third centuries A.D. by
some authorities, do contain statements pejorative in nature with
respect to Ethiopians. The books in question and relevant
passages are: Acts of Peter, 305; Acts of Andrew, 400; and Acts
of Thomas, 475, and 478.

Interpretation in Church Fathers

As Jack P. Lewis notes: "Though there are many paral-
lels in the interpretation of the flood between the rabbis and the
church fathers, it is in the spiritual interpretation that they went
their separate ways."[22] However, with Irenaeus (A.D. 185) we
begin to see the influence of the Septuagint, and of the rabbinical

----

20. *Midrash Rabbah, Genesis*, 184.

21. The source here used is Edgar Hennecke, comp., *New Testament Aprocrypha*, ed. W.
Schneemelcher, English trans., R. McL Wilson, vol. 1, *Gospels and Related Writings*; vol. 2,
Writings Relating to the Apostles, Apocalypses and Related Subjects (Philadelphia: The
Westminster Press, 1963, 1965).

22. Lewis, 156.

interpretation upon Gentile Christians wherein the curse of Canaan is transformed into a curse upon Ham, although with no reference as yet to color.[23] Origen, Jerome, Augustine, and others down to the seventh century interpret the Old Testament references to Black persons and peoples frequently but in an allegorical and typological manner.[24] Although Ham is not yet black, Origen does associate Ethiopians with Ham.[25] And Jerome, who shows in his letters a dreadful aversion to black Ethiopians,[26] translates, for the first time according to Frank M. Snowden, Jr., the conjunction in Song of Songs 1:5 as *but* rather than as *and*.[27]

Origen, it is said, set the pattern for Patristic interpretation, so we cite some of his interpretations by way of example, as they are treated by Snowden in his book *Blacks in Antiquity*. Snowden calls attention to the fact that early Christian writers, when commenting upon a given Scriptural passage involving Ethiopians, developed a type of exegesis which collated several familiar references to Ethiopians. And, with reference to Origen, he writes as follows:

> Origen says that several passages suggest themselves to him as being in accordance with 'I am black and beautiful.' In this connection Origen first cites with brief comment and then presents a detailed exegesis of the following: (1) Moses' marriage to the Ethiopian woman; (2) the visit of the Queen of Sheba to Solomon; (3) "Ethiopia shall stretch out her hand to God;" (4) "from beyond the rivers of Ethiopia will I receive my dispersed ones; they shall bring me sacrifice"; (5) the Ethiopian eunuch Abdimelech.[28]

---

23. Ibid, 119.

24. See Lewis for *typological* interpretation and Snowden for *allegorical* interpretation.

25. Snowden, 202.

26. For Jerome's attitude, see Jean Devisse and Michel Mollat, *The Image of The Black In Western Art*, vol. 2, trans. William G. Ryan (New York: William Morrow & Company, Inc., 1979) 256, 299, note 1.

27. Snowden, 198.

28. Ibid, 201.

Snowden then proceeds to give Origen's detailed allegorical exegesis of the passages. And, in describing part of the Song of Solomon 1:5, he notes that Origen makes, among others, the following points which appear in similar or modified form in commenting on the words of the Bride to the young maidens of Jerusalem: (1) the Bride who speaks represents the Church gathered from among the Gentiles; (2) her body, black externally, lacks neither natural beauty nor that acquired by practice; (3) the daughters of an earthly Jerusalem, upon seeing the Church of the Gentiles, despise her because she cannot boast the noble blood of Abraham, Isaac, and Jacob; (4) the Bride's reply is that she is black and that though she cannot point to descent from illustrious men, she is nevertheless beautiful, for in her is the image of God and she has received her beauty from the word of God; (5) she is black by reason of her lowly origin but is beautiful through penitence and faith; (6) the daughters of Jerusalem in reproaching her on account of her blackness should not forget what Mary (Miriam) suffered when she spoke against Moses because he had married a black Ethiopian woman.[29]

Over against Origen and others who followed an allegorical and typological method in treating the Black peoples in the Old Testament—members of the "Alexandrian School" of interpretation—stand the members of the "Antiochan School" who employed a literal method of exegesis. It is interesting to view the manner in which a member of this school deals with the same passage, not only in order to see Biblical interpretation but also how some people in that period regarded the *Egyptians* with respect to color, just as St. Augustine refers to the Ethiopians as black in his commentary on the Psalms. For an example I take Theodore of Mopseustia whom Robert M. Grant calls the greatest interpreter of the school of Antioch. Grant discusses Theodore's dealing with the Song of Songs as follows:

> Theodore's analysis of the Song of Songs is interesting....Its historical occasion is the wedding of Solomon with the daughter of Pharaoh. At this point in his discussion a certain sense of decorum overcomes Theodore, and he insists that the wedding took place not for pleasure, but for the political stability of Israel. Moreover, since the princess was black and therefore not especially

---

29. Ibid, 199.

attractive to the court of Solomon, he built a palace
for her and composed this song—so that she would
not be irritated and so that enmity would not arise
between him and Pharaoh.[30]

Interpretation in Targums

Martin McNamara in his book *Targum* and *Testament*
takes note that Pseudo-Jonathan on Numbers 12:1 explains that
Moses was constrained against his will to marry the Ethiopian
woman and that he later divorced her.   Further, McNamara
observes that Targum Onkelos paraphrases "Cushite" as
"beautiful"; and that other texts of the Palestinian Targum retain
the word "Cushite" but go on to explain at length that she was
not a Cushite ethnically speaking, but merely like a Cushite in
complexion![31]   Henry S. Noerdlinger in his *Moses and Egypt*
explains that the depiction of Moses' wife as white in the movie
"Ten Commandments" was based upon rabbinic traditions, as
reported in L. Ginzberg's *Legends Of The Jews* (VI:90).
According to the rabbinic tradition referred to, "Ethiopian," with
reference to Moses' wife, means that she distinguished herself
from others by her beauty and virtue, just as an Ethiopian
distinguishes himself from others by his physical appearance.[32]
In his book *Ethiopia and The Bible*, Edward Ullendorff makes
reference to an ancient Gematria employed by the Targum which
renders Cushite woman as beautiful woman, and in so doing calls
attention to Rashi.[33]

Interpretation in Muslim Writings

Although no curse of Ham or Canaan by which the one or
the other was turned black appears in the Koran, Muslim

----
30. Robert M. Grant, *The Bible In The Church*: *A Short History of Interpretation* (New York:
Macmillan Co., 1948), 77f.

31. Martin McNamara, *Targum and Testament* (Grand Rapids, Mich.: William B. Eerdmans
Publishing Co., 1972), 72.

32. Henry S. Noerdlinger, *Moses and Egypt* (Los Angeles: University of Southern California
Press, 1956), 70.

33. Edward Ullendorff, *Ethiopia and The Bible*, The Schweich Lectures (1967) (London:
Published for The British Academy by Oxford University Press, 1968), 8.

interpreters borrowed heavily from the Jews, and added some of their own. In this connection Bernard Lewis writes that a common explanation of the slave status of the black man among Muslims is that the ancestor of the dark-skinned people was Ham the son of Noah who (according to Muslim legend) was damned black for his sin. The curse of blackness, and with it that of slavery, passed to all black peoples who are his descendants.[34] In agreement with Lewis' observation on Ham's blackness among Muslims is the *Shorter Encyclopedia of Islam* which alludes to Midrash Rabbah Genesis.[35]

Jewish-Christian Interpretation During the Middle Ages

Jewish interpretation continued throughout the Middle Ages in the form of midrashim, targumim, and commentaries, all dealing with a curse on a black Ham or Canaan, with Black Biblical characters, and with those made black by the earlier interpretations in Midrashim and Talmuds. By way of example, a Midrash on the Song of Solomon, dated by W.O.E. Oesterly and G.H. Box around A.D 750, but containing very early material, interprets verse 1:5 allegorically thus: "I appear black in my deeds, but comely in those of my fathers. The congregation of Israel says, I appear black unto myself, but comely in the eyes of my Creator."[36]

Further, in the midrashic collection known as *The Book of Yasher* one finds, as presented by the translator-editor, the following account of Moses' marriage to an Ethiopian princess—an account much like that given by Josephus:

> So Moses took the city by his wisdom, and the children of Cush set him on the throne...And they...gave him Queen Adonijah the Cushite...to wife. But Moses feared the Lord...and he went not

---

34. Bernard Lewis, *Race And Color In Islam* (New York: Harper & Row, Torchbooks, 1971), 66f. The very same statement appears in Graham W. Irwin, *Africans Abroad* (New York: Columbia University Press, 1977), 128. Lewis depends heavily upon Gustave E. von Grunebaum, *Medieval Islam: A Study In Cultural Orientation* (Chicago: The University of Chicago Press, 1946).

35. *Shorter Encyclopedia of Islam*, 1974 ed., s.v. "Nuh."

36. W.O.E. Oesterly and G.H. Box, *A Short Survey Of The Literature of Rabbinical and Medieval Judaism* (New York: Macmillian Co., 1920; repr., New York: Burt Franklin, 1973), 76.

in unto her...For Moses remembered how Abraham
had made Eliezer his servant swear, saying: "Take
not a wife of the daughters of Canaan, nor shalt
thou make marriages with any of the children of
Ham..."[37]

Saadya Gaon (892-942) translated the Hebrew Bible into
Arabic, and in so doing made Noah's curse rest upon Ham rather
that upon Canaan. This act added fuel to the fire that had been
started with the same translation in the one manuscript of the
Septuagint.[38]

Greatest of all the Medieval Jewish commentators was
Rabbi Solomon ben Isaac of Troyes, better known as Rashi
(1040-1105). In his treatment of Noah's curse he refers to the
interpretation given in Midrash Rabbah-Genesis and other works
prior to his time.

Hugo Fuchs notes that Rashi makes use of Targum
Onkelos and of oral interpretation in his commentary on the
Torah.[39] And with specific reference to Rashi's interpretation on
Moses' Cushite wife, D.S. Margolioux, who calls Rashi's
interpretation "frivolous," notes that it is as old as Targum
Onkelos.[40]

Commenting on Rashi's influence upon the Christian
world, Isadore Epstein writes: "Nicholas de Lyra (1265-1349),
who is an important link between the Middle Ages and the
Reformation, quotes Rashi constantly in his Commentaries,
which, in turn, was one of the main sources used by Luther in his
translation; and many of Rashi's interpretations entered into the
King James version of the Bible."[41]

----

37. Ben Zion Halper, ed. and trans., *Post-Biblical Hebrew Literature: An Anthology*
(Philadelphia: The Jewish Publication Society of America, 1921), 132ff.

38. For references to Ham as the accursed one in an Arabic Bible,, see Adam Clarke, *The Holy
Bible*, with a commentary and critical notes, vol. 1 (Nashville: Abingdon Press, n.d.), 38; Josiah
Priest, *Slavery As It Relates To The Negro, Or African Race* (Albany, New York: C. van
Benthuysen and Co., 1843; repr., Albany, New York: Arno Press., Inc., 1977), 77ff.; and
Custance, 25.

39. *The Universal Jewish Encyclopedia*, 1954 ed., s.v. "Rashi," by Hugo Fuchs. H. Wheeler
Robinson, ed., *The Bible In Its Ancient and English Versions* (Oxford: Oxford University Press,
1940; repr., Oxford: Claredon Press, 1954) 147, notes that Lyra made literal translation of
Rashi's commentary that preserved the Rabbinical tradition of the Middle Ages into modern
times.

40. *A Dictionary Of The Bible*, 1911 ed., vol. 1, s.v. "Ethiopian Woman."

41. Isadore Epstein, *Judaism: A Historical Presentation* (Baltimore, Md.: Penguin Books Inc.,
1959), 269.

According to Louis Ginzberg, there is no evidence for the direct use of rabbinic literature by the Christian world before the twelfth century,[42] and this is the very time of Rashi.

At least by the twelfth century in Europe, Cain is depicted with Negroid features in art as well as in literature.[43] Such a depiction may well go back to as early as Beowulf who makes mention of Cain's monstrous descendants. Quite interestingly, Cain's black color is attributed to more than the occasion of his sacrifice as in Genesis Rabbah. It comes to be attributed additionally to a curse because of his murder of Abel, and to the mark or sign that God placed upon him for his protection. Whatever the time and whatever the cause of Cain's being turned black, Cain as black became associated with Black peoples in the minds of Europeans as well as Jews and the association is in the minds of Europeans and their descendants world-wide today.

Despite the anti-blackness among Jews and Gentile Europeans with which we have dealt, it must be recognized that for a time and in different parts of Europe the Ethiopian received favorable regard. The most that can be done in this lecture to support this view is to refer to the three-volume work by Jean Devisse and Michel Mollat, *The Image Of The Black In Western Art*, and Joseph R. Washington, Jr's, recent book, *Anti-Blackness In English Religion*.[44]

Towards the end of the Middle Ages, the anti-black influence of Jewish interpretation on that of Gentile Christian Europeans may be noted in the writings of Sir John Mandeville who in 1336 refashioned the story of Ham. Although he views Ham as the accursed one, he regards him as the mightiest and richest of Noah's three sons.[45]

Interpretation in Modern Times

The fifteenth century, which saw the importation of West African Blacks into Europe in ever increasing numbers, marks

----

42. Louis Ginzberg, *On Jewish Law and Lore* (Philadelphia: The Jewish Publication Society of America, 1955), 67.

43. See Ruth Mellinkoff, *The Mark of Cain* (Los Angeles: University of California Press, 1981), 76ff.

44. Joseph R. Washington, Jr., *Anti-Blackness In English Religion: 1500-1800* (New York: The Edwin Mellen Press, 1984). See note 26.

45. Ibid, 42f.

the real beginning of the application of the Ham-Canaan-Cain accounts to Black peoples, as interpreted by the Jews. One of the first to make such application was Gomes Eannes Zurara, chronicler for Prince Henry the Navigator. Confusing Cain with Noah's cursed son, in his history on the discovery of Guinea, Zurara wrote:

> You must note that these Blacks were Moors like the others, but were their slaves, in accordance with ancient custom, which I believe to have been because of the curse which, after the Deluge, Noah laid upon his son Cain [sic], cursing him in this way: that his race should be subject to all other races of the world.[46]

From this time, forward, notes Ronald Sanders, in his book, *Lost Tribes And Promised* Lands, Noah's curse will serve as a standard excuse for Black slavery among Europeans as it had for Moslems.[47]

A view aberrant from those that held Blacks to be offspring of Ham-Canaan-Cain entered the picture with Paracelsus (1520), who expressed the opinion that Negroes and some others had a separate origin from those who had descended from Adam. This opinion would be adopted and elaborated upon by many who would come later.[48]

Returning to the curse of Ham/Canaan in the various and proliferating interpretations given to it, positive and negative, note may be taken of a sixteenth century writer on the subject, George Best (1577). Relying upon Jewish interpretations well known by this time, and adding something new of his own, Best wrote concerning Ham and his descendants:

> God would a sonne should be born whose name was Chus, who not onely it selfe, but all his posterite after him should bee so blacke and loathsome, that it might remaine a spectacle of disobedience to all the

----
46. Quoted in Ronald Sanders, *Lost Tribes and Promised Lands* (Boston: Little, Brown and Co., 1978), 62.

47. Ibid, 63.

48. For aberrant views of Paracelsus and others, see Thomas F. Gossett, *Race: The History of An Idea In America* (Dallas, Texas: Southern Methodist University Press, 1963; New York: Schocken Books, 1963), 15.

worlde.   And of this blacke and cursed Cush came
all these blacke Moores, which are in Africa....[49]

Winthrop J. Jordan notes that Ham's curse became
common in the seventeenth century as an explanation of the
Negro's color rather than as a support for slavery.[50] And David
Brion Davis observes a probable increasing tendency around 1676
for Americans to identify Negroes with the children of Ham.[51]
This tendency, however, was contrary to the views of Sir Thomas
Browne (1605-1682) and many others who attributed the color to
natural causes.   Jordan regards Browne as the bridge between
Medieval and modern times with respect to the Negro's color;[52]
and from his time onwards the matter will be discussed and
debated until at last Ham's-Canaan's curse, with or without the
questionable *curse*, *mark* or *sacrifice* of Cain, will be used to
justify Black slavery, and still later, segregation.
   While still in the seventeenth century, it must be noted
that the aberrant view of Paracelsus in 1520 was developed
further by Issac de la Peyere. This author in 1655 wrote that the
natives of Africa, Asia, and the New World were descendants
from a Pre-Adamite race. According to him, it was from this
race that Cain had chosen a wife, a view that will later be
expanded upon until that wife comes to be designated a Negro
woman.[53]
   During the whole of the 1700's, as has been anticipated,
debate continued with respect to Ham and Canaan, as well as
with respect to Cain as black. In the year 1700 Judge Samuel
Sewall in his famous work *The Selling Of Joseph* argued against
an opponent that the curse on Canaan had been fulfilled in the
enslavement of the Gibeonites.[54]   Nevertheless,   according to

----

49. Quoted in Washington, 114; Winthrop D. Jordan, *White Over Black*: *American Attitudes
Toward The Negro, 1550-1812* (Chapel Hill, North Carolina: University of North Carolina
Press, 1968), 41; Sanders, 224 and in other publications.

50. Jordan, 18.

51. David Brion Davis, *The Problem of Slavery In Western Culture* (Ithaca, New York: Cornell
University Press, 1966), 316f.

52. Jordan, 15ff.

53. Information concerning Peyere and his views is obtainable from encyclopedias and from
popular writings such as those of Gossett, 15; Sabine Baring-Gould, *Legends of The Patriarchs
and Prophets* (New York: Hurst & Co., n.d.), 26f.; Don Cameron Allen, *The Legend Of Noah*
(Urban, Ill.: University of Illinois Press, 1963), 86f.

David Brion Davis, by 1733 there was an increasing tendency to identify Negroes not only as children of Ham but also of Cain.[55]

Elihu Coleman (1699-1789) pointed out that Negroes could not be the posterity of Cain because all his descendants had perished in the flood, as others after him will continue to do, while still others, of an opposite mind, will develop views that will link Ham even with a daughter of Cain.[56] The wide currency of views with regard to Cain and blackness, again whether based upon his sacrifice, murder of Abel, or mark, may be observed as they existed at the end of the eighteenth century and the early years of the nineteenth in the writings of Phyllis Wheatley and David Walker, respectively. In her poem "On Being Brought From Africa To America" Phyllis writes:

"Twas mercy brought me from my Pagan land.
Taught my benighted soul to understand.
That there's a God, that there's a Saviour too.
Once I redemption neither sought nor knew.
Some view our sable race with scornful eye,
'Their color is a diabolic die.'
Remember, Christians, Negroes, *black as Cain*,
May be refined, and join th' angelic train.[57]

On the other hand, David Walker in his *Appeal* lambasts Whites for calling Black people the seed of Cain, informing them that he has read his Bible too without finding such a reference there. Not finding it in his Bible, Walker turns the tables and accuses White people of being those who are Cain's seed.[58]

As has been anticipated, once more, the nineteenth century saw continuing debates, especially about the Ham-Canaan curse, but with increasing fury as pro-slavery and anti-slavery writers contested with each other. In a general way we may here

----

54. See Davis, 316ff.: Louis Ruchames, ed., *Racial Thought In America*, vol. 1 *From The Puritans to Abraham Lincoln*: *A Documentary History* (Amhurst, Mass.: University of Massachusetts Press, 1969; New York: Gossett and Dunlap, 1970), 46ff.

55. Davis, ibid.

56. Ruchames, 89ff.

57. Quoted in Alan Lomax and Raoul Abdul, eds., *3000 Years of Black Poetry* (New York: Dodd, Mead & Co., 1970), 205.

58. David Walker, *Walker's Appeal In Four Articles* (1829), repr., with a new preface by William Loren Katz (New York: Arno Press and The New York Times, 1969), 71ff.

cite several of the numerous views and counter-views that were propounded:[59] 1) the old curse of Ham-Canaan doctrine with no reference to the achievements of Hamites as presented in Genesis, chapter 10; 2) a curse of Canaan view that held only Canaan was cursed, and with attention paid to the sons of Ham as founders of ancient civilizations in Africa and Asia; 3) a new view that Ham had been born black, was later cursed outright, and that all his descendants partake of the curse; 4) a view that Cain, Ham, and Canaan were all tied together, making for a three-fold curse on Black peoples; 5) a new view that there was and is no curse upon Ham and his descendants, and that Canaan instead of having been black was white; 6) a resurrected Pre-Adamite view that forged a link with a theory of polygenesis and removed the Negro from the Adamic-Noahite human family and declared him a beast; 7) a view that held Negroes to be descendants of Adam-Noah, accepted Genesis, chapter 10, as referring to Black folk, and took note that Jesus was a colored man; 8) a multiple view that combined the whole or parts of several anti-Negro views; 9) a new and increasingly accepted view—a new Hamite doctrine, contributed to and accepted by the rising critical historical-literary study of the Bible, that removed Blacks from the Bible altogether. According to this last view, Ham and all his descendants were white.[60]

All the afore-listed views, plus still others, continued on into the twentieth century with greater or lesser strength, varying according to different groups. And although the anti-Negro views might not have been as loudly voiced during the present century until 1954 and afterwards, they were hardly asleep. They were only dozing. The attention paid especially to the curse of Ham during the intervening years, even among mainline White denominations, was great, indeed!

As is quite well known, the Supreme Court decision of 1954, relative to separate and equal education, stabbed fully awake the anti-Negro Cain-Ham-Canaan views. On the other hand, it stirred into action advocates of the new Hamite

---

59. T. Peterson, "*The Myth of Ham Among White Antebellum Southerners*, " (PH.D. diss., Stanford University, 1975); 146, isolates four versions of the Ham Myth among Southern White Americans.

60. For a statement of this view, see William F. Albright, "The Old Testament World," in *The Interpreter's Bible*, George Arthur Buttrick, Commentary Editor (New York: Abingdon-Cokesbury Press, 1952), vol. 1, 233-277. See also Paul Heinisch, *History of The Old Testament*, trans. William G. Heidt (Collegeville, Minn.: The Order of St. Benedict, Inc., 1952), 52.

doctrine. These latter, more or less sympathetic towards Blacks, did battle with protagonists for the old view.

Only in passing can we observe that after 1954, pro-segregationists revived every pro-slavery argument based upon Ham-Canaan-Cain in support of segregation. Such arguments continue today among some sects, some television ministries, and among such groups as the Ku Klux Klan.

On the other hand, some mainline White denominations have produced literature in refutation particularly of the Ham-Canaan doctrine. And several individual authors wrote similar books on the subject of segregation and the Bible. Such are the books *Segregation And The Bible* by Everett Tilson,[61] and *Segregation And Scripture* by J. Oliver Buswell III.[62] Both the denominational literature and the books were written from the position of the new Hamite doctrine which, as we have seen does not view Blacks (Negroes) as having been among the peoples of the Biblical world; and thus not subjects in the Biblical accounts about Cain, Ham, Canaan, or any other Biblical character.

To be noted also is the fact that in 1978 the Mormon Church admitted Blacks to the priesthood, thus removing, apparently, Negroes from a curse on Cain-Ham-Canaan?

In recent years a new and unique interpretation has been presented by a Canadian scholar, Arthur C. Custance. He regards the Genesis Table of Nations as historically trustworthy, and tradition-wise believes that Noah's three sons represent the three racial groups that make up the world's people. To the Shemites, he assigns Hebrews, Arabs, Babylonians, Assyrians, etc.; to the Japhethites, those whom he calls Caucasoids; and to the Hamites he assigns the Mongoloid and Negroid peoples. He then suggests that the curse that was pronounced upon Canaan or upon Ham should be interpreted to mean a servant "par excellence," i.e., the servants would perform a great service to their brethren.[63]

Biblical Interpretation by Black Peoples

Up to this point reference has been made to only two Black popular interpreters. We turn now to view the subject as

----

61. Everett Tilson, *Segregation and The Bible* (New York: Abingdon press,, 1958).

62. J. Oliver Buswell, *Segregation and Scripture* (Grand Rapids, Mich.: William B. Eerdmans Publishing Co., 1964).

63. Custance, 120, 149.

dealt with by Black peoples themselves. With respect to written documents one may go back to the year 1742 and the person of Jacob Elisa Capitein (1717-1742), then to Jupiter Hammond in 1760, and then continue in an unbroken line to the present.[64]

In his booklet, *The Redemption Of Africa and Black Religion*, St. Clair Drake paints a beautiful picture of early Black Biblical interpretation by both literate and illiterate preachers, and by those whom he calls folk theologians. Ignoring Capitein, who aped the White pro-slavery advocates, Drake says that preachers and theologians were able to counterattack White anti-Black interpretation by invalidating Noah's curse. They insisted that the curse had been wiped out with the coming of Christ, or by arguing that God is the father of all men and that all men are brothers. Further, they were able to point to the Black peoples in the Bible (using the Genesis Table of Nations), and to individual Black characters in the Bible, and glory in a great past history.[65]

True as Mr. Drake's picture may appear on the surface, it does not represent the painting in its entirety. The literature from 1742 to the present, as well as oral responses, reveals responses and interpretations relative to the curse of Ham-Canaan if not with respect to a curse upon Cain. These responses and interpretations range all the way from unquestioning acceptance, to ignorance about it, through uncertainty, to scornful rejection.

With such a general preliminary observation having been made, I shall deal first with Black reaction to, if not Black interpretation of, a curse upon Cain. Of Phyllis Wheatley's acceptance and David Walker's rejection note already has been taken. Forty-five years after David Walker, in 1874, William Wells Brown wrote that Cain's curse as related to color was nothing more than speculation that falls to the ground when we trace back the genealogy of Noah, finding that he descended not from Cain but from Seth.[66] Nothing more appears about Cain in the writings of Black authors until the year 1883. In that year

---

64. Accounts of Capitein may be found in Henri Gregoire, *An Enquiry Concerning the Intellectual and Moral Faculties and Literature of Negroes*, trans. D.B. Warden (Brooklyn, New York: Thomas Kirk, 1810; repr., College Park, Maryland: McGrath Publishing Co., 1967), 196-202; J.C. de Graft-Johnson, *African Glory* (New York: Walker & Co., 1954), 158ff.; and Johannes Verkuyl, *Break Down The Walls*, ed. and trans. Lewis B. Smedes (Grand Rapids, Mich.: William B. Eerdmans Publishing Co., 1973), 31f.

65. St. Clair Drake, *The Redemption of Africa and Black Redemption* (Chicago: Third World Press, 1970), 48.

66. William Wells Brown, *The Rising Son* (Boston: A.G. Brown & Co., 1874; repr., New York: Negro Universities Press, 1970), 46-47.

George Washington Williams published his *History Of The Negro Race from 1619 to 1880* in which he expresses the opinion that even among White people it had died out as an explanation of the Negro's color.[67] Indeed, it does appear to have died out among Black people in America even if it had not among Whites. By 1883 the Mormons had crystallized the curse or mark upon Cain as referring to Black peoples as a doctrine. Later Black writers have referred to it only in passing.

Joel A. Rogers in his book, *Sex and Race*, published in 1944, reports, contrary to the view of the rabbis that Cain's face had turned black, that Black West Africans taught that Cain was originally black, but that when he killed Abel and God shouted at him in the garden he turned white from fright.[68] Over against this view, Marcus Garvey classified White people as descendants of Cain and Black people as the children of Abel.[69] James Baldwin, speaking for at least some Black people, states that just as we knew Blacks were in the eyes of White people cursed descendants of Ham, so *for us* White people were the descendants of Cain.[70] Olin P. Moyd makes reference to this report by Baldwin in his book, *Redemption in Black Theology*, published in 1979.[71] And between Baldwin and Moyd, George D. Kelsey, in dealing with the White racist views of the late Reverend Dr. G. G. Gillespie who had included the mark of Cain in comments about Negroes, made reference to it, 1965.[72] Finally, Latta R. Thomas (1976) quotes David Walker's statement,[73] and Carl F. Ellis, Jr. refers to the mark of Cain as a myth.[74]

----

67. George Washington Williams, *History Of The Negro Race In America From 1619 to 1880* (New York: G.P. Putnam's Sons, 1883; repr., New York: Arno Press and The New York Times, 1968), vol 1, 19.

68. Joel A. Rogers, *Sex and Race*, 5th ed.(New York: Helga M.Rogers, 1944,1972), vol.3, 317.

69. Amy Jacques-Garvey, ed., *Philosophy and Opinions of Marcus Garvey*, with a new preface by William Loren Katz (New York: Arno Press and The New York Times, 1969), 412.

70. James Baldwin, *The Fire Next Time* (New York: Dell Publishing Co., 1962), 59.

71. Olin P. Moyd, *Redemption in Black Theology* (Valley Forge, Pa.: Judson Press, 1979), 154ff.

72. George D. Kelsey, *Racism and The Christian Understanding of Man* (New York: Charles Scribner's Sons, 1965), 26.

73. Latta R. Thomas, *Biblical Faith and the Black Man* (Valley Forge, Pa.: Judson Press, 1976), 49.

74. Carl F. Ellis, *Beyond Liberation* (Downer's Grove, Ill.: Inter Varsity Press, 1983), 41.

A discussion of Black interpretations of the Ham-Canaan curse might well continue with the observation that up to a generation ago Black writers boasted proudly of Negroes' being the children of Ham.[75] They either by-passed, hid, or ignored the curse and emphasized, usually, as Drake points out, the glorious record of the children of Ham as set forth in the tenth chapter of Genesis. Additionally, great emphasis was placed upon Psalm 68 with its assertion that Ethiopia would stretch forth her hands to God.[76] And Drake's observation has been applicable especially down to 1900.

In reviewing publications by Black writers from 1837 to 1902, one notes that, with few exceptions, every Black writer dealt with a glorious, ancient Black history, based upon the Bible which was viewed as factual. Thus so spoke and wrote the Reverend H. Easton in 1837; James W.C. Pennington in 1841; R.B. Lewis in 1844; Henry H. Garnett in 1848; Martin R. Delany in 1952; Alexander Crumwell in 1862; William Wells Brown again in 1874; George Washington Williams in 1883; Edwards A. Johnson in 1891; Rufus L. Perry in 1893; Benjamin T. Tanner in 1902; and J.J. Pipkin in 1902. All these were Afro-Americans; all were traditionalists in their view of the Bible. Interestingly enough, the works of Perry and Tanner were written partly to refute the Hamite doctrine that removed Blacks from the Bible.[77]

For some Africans who lived in the period just surveyed in America, interpretation of the old Hamite doctrine was not so healthfully handled. Claude Wauthier reports that as early as 1870, at the first Vatican Council, a group of missionary bishops produced a document asking the Pope to release the Negro race from the curse which, it seems, comes from Ham.[78]

Shortly after 1902, and continuing to the present, there are to be found Black writers of Black history based upon the Bible. Most of these have been traditionalist and fundamentalist, unacquainted with or unaccepting of modern historical-literary Biblical studies. On the other hand, there has arisen an increasing number of Black Biblical scholars who are trained in

----

75. The number of Black writers who did so is legion.

76. See Drake, and Gayraud S. Wilmore, *Black Religion and Black Radicalism* (Garden City, New York: Doubleday & Co., 1972), 166ff.

77. Speeches and books by the authors named are quite easily obtainable.

78. Claude Wauthier, *The Literature & Thought of Modern Africa*, trans. Shirley Kay (New York: Praeger Publishers, 1967), 209.

critical exegetical methods, and who are interpreting the Bible from a Black perspective, and giving instructions to others on how to interpret the Bible through the use of critical methodologies. Among such scholars are Bishop Alfred G. Dunston, Jr., the Reverend Jacob Dyer, Dr. Robert A. Bennett, and the Reverend Latta Thomas. This last author urges Blacks to hold on the Biblical faith despite such interpretations as those that insist upon a curse upon Ham. [79]

In Africa, the late Cheikh Anta Diop presented a non-traditional and critical treatment of the "Ham Legend" in his book *The African Origin of Civilization: Myth or Reality?*[80] And E. Mveng of Cameroun treats what he calls the "Myth of Ham" in an article entitled "The Bible And Black Africa."[81]

Not to be excluded in a lecture of this kind is an aberrant type of Black Biblical interpretation that has existed for some two generations and is increasing among several groups. This type goes beyond Black identification of Black peoples with the Biblical Hamites and claims that Black peoples are to be identified with the ancient Jews; or with the ancient Hebrew-Israelites, as different from Jews of modern times. For these the Old Testament especially is a collection of writings by and about Black peoples.[82]

Conclusion

Thus we come to the end of our general survey of three thousand years of Biblical interpretation with reference to Black peoples. The survey has shown that the most probable original

---

79. The authors referred to and the titles of their works are as follows: Alfred G. Dunston, Jr., *The Black Man In The Old Testament and Its World* (Philadelphia: Dorrance & Co., 1974); Robert A. Bennett, "Biblical Hermeneutics and The Black Preacher, *"The Journal of The Interdenominational Theological Center*, Vol.I, No.II, (Spring 1974): pages 38-53; Jacob A. Dyer, *The Ethiopian in the Bible* (New York: Vantage Press, 1974); Latta R. Thomas, *Biblical Faith and the Black American* (Valley Forge: Judson Press, 1976).

80. Cheikh Anta Diop, *The African Origin of Civilization: Myth or Reality?* ed. and trans. Mercer Cook (New York: Lawrence Hill & Co., 1974), 245ff.

81. E. Mveng, "La Bible Et L'Afrique Noire," *Proceedings of The Jerusalem Congress on Black Africa and The Bible, April 14-30*, 1972, eds. E. Mveng and R.J.Z. Werblowsky, (n.p.).

82. Among those that identify with the Biblical Jews are Black Jewish groups such as Church of God and Saints of Christ; Commandment Keepers Congregation, alternately known as Royal Order of Ethiopian Jews; and the Black Christian Nationalist Movement of the Reverend Albert C. Cleague, Jr. Identifying with the Hebrews-Israelites as distinct from Jews is the Original Hebrew Israelite Nation of Jerusalem. A rather voluminous body of literature concerning these groups now exists.

text of the Hebrew was free of perjortive statements with respect to peoples regarded as black by the original authors; and that, with one or two possible exceptions, the same holds true of inner-Biblical interpretation. Further, it has revealed that apart from extra-Biblical interpretation by the ancient rabbis and others like them, whose interpretations appear in Midrashim, Talmuds, haggadah, and targumim, there are no curses upon Cain, Ham, Canaan, whereby they were cursed with blackness. Again, it has noted that early Gentile Christians failed to adopt the anti-Black interpretations of the Jews, while the Muslims did; and that later, Gentile Christians, particularly in Europe, adopted the interpretations and applied them to Black peoples whom they met in increasing numbers. And so it has continued unto this day. On the other hand, the survey has gone on to reveal that Black peoples, at times ambivalent, in the main have managed to invalidate the White interpretations of the old anti-Black Hamite doctrine; and at points have challenged the new Hamite view that removes Blacks from the Bible.

Two concluding observations may be attempted. Inasmuch as a curse of blackness whether upon Cain, or Ham, or Canaan does not appear in the Biblical text, those who take the Bible, including the Old Testament to be the Word of God, norm for faith and practice, would appear to be engaging in blasphemy when they substitute interpretations. Secondly, according to numerous Jewish scholars, many White Gentile Christians during modern times, and an increasing number of enlightened Black Biblical scholars, the interpretations of the ancient Jewish rabbis are to be classified as legends and myths. Thus, legend and myth have been made to serve as actual historical fact to the damnation of Black peoples, except where Black peoples have believed and acted otherwise.

Chapter 8

Racial Myths and
Biblical Scholarship

Some Random Notes and Observations

Despite the fact that some scholars of renown are of the opinion that racial/color prejudice did not exist in the ancient world (D.J. Wiseman, ed., *Peoples of Old Testament*, pp. xix f.; A.S. Van Der Woude, gen. ed., *The World Of the Bible*, p. 344; Frank M. Snowden, Jr., *Before Color Prejudice*; etc.) there is evidence that throughout the ages, since Biblical times, a great deal of Biblical interpretation has been and still is based upon certain so-called myths employed by Biblical scholars, especially with reference to Blacks/Negroes. Hence a close association between racial myths and at least some Biblical scholarship.

In these random notes I have jotted down in more or less outline form, examples of Biblical interpretation that have employed myths, and at points have made observations and comments. The notes begin with what today would definitely be termed racial myths, myths created and employed by the first interpreters of the so-called Old Testament, the ancient Jewish rabbis. They then continue through the use of myths inherited from the rabbis, supplemented by myths created and used by interpreters of the Bible in modern times, then deal with Biblical interpretations that demonstrate some of the specific myths that govern the interpretation of some interpreters.

The creation and employment of racial/color myths by Biblical scholars characterize the very beginning of Biblical interpretation with particular reference to Black People. Such was the interpretation of the ancient Jewish rabbis in their interpretation of the Cain story, and in their interpretation of the curse upon Canaan, transformed into a curse upon Ham and/or upon his descendants. Thus Cain was said to have been turned black when smoke from his unacceptable sacrifice blew back upon him (*Midrash Rabbah-Genesis XXII: 5-6*). Thus also was Ham cursed with blackness for a variety of reasons (myth), including his having shown disrespect for his drunken, naked father; having copulated in the Ark, etc., and his descendants cursed to be black and slaves after him (*Babylonian Talmud, Sanhedrin* 108b; *Midrash Rabbah-Genesis* XXXVI: 7-8 etc.). The several and various versions of the curse of Ham Myth may be subsumed under the one heading of the Old Hamite Myth in view of the fact that in modern times there arose another myth based upon the Ham story that is referred to as *The New Hamite Myth*. (See the unpublished Thesis of Edith R. Sanders entitled *The Hamites In Anthropology and History: A Preliminary Study*.)

As is well known, the Old Hamite Myth was used by Jews down through the ages, and was adopted by Euro-American interpreters of the Bible to justify the enslavement and later segregation of the Negroes. With reference to White Gentile employment of the myth, excluding such persons as St. Jerome who found Blacks repulsive, as indicated in part by his translation of Song of Songs 1:5-6, it appears that the early Church Fathers escaped pejorative interpretations of passages that refer to Blacks by their use of allegorical and typological methods in interpretation. Latter day White Christian Scholars, especially after 1450, when West African Blacks became commonplace, made use of the Jewish interpretations, and created new, additional ones of their own. Going beyond the use of Cain-Ham-Canaan myths, some developed a Pre-Adamite myth that removed Negroes and other non-Europeans from the families of Adam-Noah.

Around 1800, and related to Napoleon's invasion of Egypt in 1798, there was born the New Hamite Myth. In its origins it was designed particularly to prove that, contrary to ancient writers such as Herodotus, the ancient Egyptians were not Blacks/Negroes. It continued to grow and mature during the 19th century so that by the time critical historical-literary methodology reached maturity at the end of the century it too had arrived at full development; and it has had great influence upon Biblical Scholarship.

As related to the social sciences in general, and to Egyptology in particular as a study ancillary to Biblical study, the New Hamite Myth removed Blacks/Negroes from the category of "civilized" altogether, and attributed all evidence of civilization among Black Africans to Hamites, all of whom were White Caucasoid-Europids even though some might literally be black in color.

Process of growth may be noted in the progressive elimination of Negroes from Egyptian history. Older historians down to the end of the century continued to regard Egyptians as having had some degree of Negroid affiliation, and called attention to the Negroid features of several pharaohs. By the time Breasted wrote his history he could declare the older historians wrong, and state that at most the ancient Egyptians had only a slight tincture of "negro" blood. (James Henry Breasted, *A History of Egypt*, second ed., fully revised, 1924, p. 26). In doing so, Breasted overlooked the fact that in America the slight tincture would cause the Egyptians still to be regarded as Negroes.

With respect to Biblical interpretation, Blacks/Negroes were removed from the Biblical World and thus from the Bible. The Hamites of the Bible were not black but white. And although the new Hamite Myth did relieve Blacks of the curse upon Ham and his descendants it nevertheless turned out, at points, to work against the Negro as much as did the older myth. In part this was due to the fact that the newer borrowed much from the older in its negative treatment of Negroes. This still proves to be true despite the fact that during the 1950s tenets of the new myth were used to show that Negroes were not under the curse of Ham/Canaan by well-meaning White Biblical Scholars. (See Everett Tilson, *Segregation and The Bible*; T.B. Maston, *Segregation and Desegregation*; *A Christian Approach*; and the footnotes related to Genesis 9:18-21, in The New American Bible, and The Living Bible).

Some results of the employment of the new myth may be observed in varying degrees in the writings for instance of Paul Heinish (*History of the Old Testament*, p. 30), Martin Noth (*The Old Testament World*, p. 236) and William F. Albright ("The Old Testament World," IB, Vol. 1, p. 238).

In dealing with the Genesis Table of Nations, Heinisch writes, "No reference is made to Indians, *Negroes*, Mongolians, Malayans, Chinese, Japanese, etc."

A little less exclusive of Negroes is Noth who gives them a role "only on the border of the Near East as neighbors of Egypt." It is to be noted that in his exclusion of Negroes Noth goes so far as to criticize the ancient Egyptians for having incorrectly depicted the Nubians as Negroes. In doing so, however, he is not being original, for he is only repeating almost verbatim an assertion made by Auguste Mariette-Bey (*The Monuments of Upper Egypt*, p.232) a hundred years previously—a time when anti-Negro interpretation of the Bible, as related to Egyptology, was reaching a peak.

Still a little less exclusive of Negroes is Albright who writes, "All known races in the region which concerns us here belonged to the so-called `white' or `Caucasian' race, with the exception of the Cushites (`Ethiopians') who were strongly Negroid in type, as we know from many Egyptians paintings."

A comparison of the opinions of Noth and Albright serves to show the confusion that exists with respect to who in the Biblical World is to be considered Black/Negro—Noth's use of the term Nubian over against Albright's use of Cushite/Ethiopian, and the inconsistencies that result.

From the foregoing discussion of the Old and New Hamite myths we turn to specific instances of the employment of racial myths by Biblical scholars in their interpretation with reference to those who in some sense are viewed as having or not having been black. We begin with interpretation of Amos 9:7. S.R. Driver (*The Books of Joel and Amos, and The Minor Prophets*) provides a *paradigm* for the use of racial myths.

In his interpretation of Amos 9:7, Driver regards the ancient Ethiopians (8th century B.C.) as a distant people, far removed from "the grace and knowledge of God," despised on account of their dark color, and perhaps on account of slaves being often drawn from them (using Jeremiah 13:23 as the basis for the view regarding color).

Similar to Driver's view is that of J.M.P. Smith in his commentary on *The Books of Amos, Hosea and Micah*, which regards the Ethiopians as far removed, and doubtless despised by Israel as black and barbarous.

That such interpretation as that by Driver and Smith is based upon myth is demonstrated by the contrary interpretation of the passage by other scholars. Thus Hughell E.W. Fosbroke in his commentary on the passage (IB, Vol.6, p. 848) takes issue with Driver, stating that the passage no more implies disdain for the Ethiopian's skin than it does for the leopard's spot, and observing further that in Isaiah 18:1-2, the Ethiopians are regarded with something akin to admiration. And Norman Snaith (*Amos, Hosea and Micah*, p. 49) can write, "The Ethiopians are named because they were a distant people of whom the Israelites would have heard. There is, of course, no slightest suggestion that the color of their skin is the point at issue; there is no warrant anywhere in the Bible for that kind of idea."

The employment of racial myth by Driver (as well as by Smith) is shown further, as we shall observe in dealing with Isaiah 18:1-2, by the fact that the ancients, if none other than the Greeks, regarded the Ethiopians as the most pious of peoples, and that the piety of the Ethiopians is aptly demonstrated by the superbly pious acts of such a ruler as Pianki. (Historians call attention to Pianki's acts.)

With special reference to Driver's having based his interpretation on an inferred disdain for Ethiopians in Jeremiah 13:23, one would have to consider the real position of Jeremiah in his relationship with Ethiopians in his day. Although their nation might still be far-distant, as a people and as individuals they were quite well known, had played an important role in the life of Judah, and in Jeremiah's own personal life.

A hundred years before Jeremiah's own times the 25th Egyptian, Ethiopian, dynasty had served as Judah's ally. And so important were they in the life of Judah that Isaiah had to warn against trusting in Egypt/Ethiopia rather than in Yahweh (Isaiah 20, 31). In Jeremiah's time Ethiopians were still on the scene in important positions—Cushites such as Zephaniah; Jehudi, grandson of one Cushi who read Jeremiah's scroll (Jeremiah 36); and Ebed-Melech, court official, who rescued the prophet from a cistern and upon whom the prophet pronounced a blessing (Jeremiah 38, 39). Unless one were to assume that Jeremiah had contempt for Ethiopians as a whole while being grateful to and blessing an individual, then Jeremiah would hardly refer to Ethiopians in a pejorative manner.

So much for Driver's views with respect to spiritual depravity and skin color of Ethiopians. With respect to slavery he assumes that Ethiopians were the only people enslaved in ancient times, when in fact, as W.G. Rollins reports (IDBS, p.830), the vast majority of slaves in those days were peoples whom today we regard as Caucasians. Or he assumes that Ethiopians were known to the ancient Hebrews-Israelites-Judahites-Jews as slaves, when in fact from most ancient times they were known as soldiers (consider the Tel el Amarna correspondence), and that still in New Testament times they were known as people of renown (consider Josephus' remarks concerning Cush, *Antiq*, I, VI).

But Driver is not alone in his opinion that the ancient Ethiopians were nothing more than slaves. In his commentary on *The Books of Samuel*, Henry P. Smith writes concerning

Ha-Cushi (II Sam. 18:21ff.): "Joab then calls a negro (naturally, a slave) and commands him: Go tell the king what thou hast seen, a message of grief by a despised messenger."

Smith then goes on to explain in a footnote that the *Cushites* were properly the Nubians but that probably the name was extended to cover all natives of Africa beyond Egypt; and that the trade in slaves brought them to Asia.

Driver's and Smith's views are shared more or less by George B. Caird (IB, 2, p.1142), and by J.M. Ward (IDBS, A-D, p. 751). Caird explains that "the Cushite was an Ethiopian, probably a slave, and so a more suitable person for the unpleasant task" of breaking the news of Absalom's death to David. With a bit more breadth of comprehension as far as possibilities are concerned, Ward refers to the CUSHITE as having been perhaps a Negro slave or a mercenary, and, as an alien, preferable to Ahimaaz as the bearer of tragic news.

Akin also to Driver's and Smith's interpretation is that of James Luther Mays in his commentary on *Amos*, p. 157. He writes,

> ...On the evidence one can say no more than that the Cushites were a distant, different folk whom Israelites knew mostly as slaves. 'You are to me,' says Yahweh, 'as these Cushites are to you.' What the comparison does is to humiliate Israel completely with respect to Yahweh, to reduce them to the role in Yahweh's order of things which the Cushites played in their own society.

In view of archaeological discoveries on the island of Crete, the presence of a Black among David's soldiers might be better explained than by having Ha-Cushi a slave, especially *naturally so*, as Smith states. If he were not a native Black Judahite, he could just as easily have been a Philistine mercenary from Crete which had received its early culture and elements in its population from Egypt and Ethiopia. (See, e.g. in part R.K. Harrison, *Old Testament Times*, p. 171 f.; especially William Lee Hansberry, *Africa & Africans As Seen by Classical Writers*, pp. 32ff.; and W.E.B. DuBois, *The World and Africa*, p. 122.)

The association of Cushites in the Bible with slaves occurs also in the treatment of Zephaniah by Aage Bentzen in his Introduction (p. 153), and by others who echo or react against his view. In commenting on Zephaniah Bentzen writes, "We do not know much of the prophet Zephaniah. His father is called Cushi, i.e. the Ethiopian, the Negro. This perhaps implies that he was of a slave family...."

Turning from Blacks as slaves, we take note of the matter of the Ethiopians' having been despised on account of their color. Here it is well not to confuse the attitudes of later Jewish rabbis with attitudes of the Hebrews-Israelite-Judahite-Jews of Biblical times, especially the times of the 8th and 7th century B.C. prophets. Interpretation of Isaiah 18:1-2 provides a good case in point with respect to scholars who do or do not follow Driver in his view with regard to color. Commenting on this passage, some scholars point to admiration for the Ethiopian's color (as does Fosbroke in his remarks), instead of disdain. Thus George B. Gray in his commentary on *Isaiah*, I-XXXIX, p. 312, referring to Herodotus' (iii:20) description of the Ethiopians "as the tallest and most beautiful of men" writes: "There is no reason why the Hebrews should not have admired the burnished copper colour of the Ethiopians, for even Jeremiah 13:23 need not be interpreted as though the ancient Hebrews shared the modern white man's objection to colour."

Almost a generation before Gray, John Skinner wrote in interpreting the passage (in his *The Book of the Prophet Isaiah*, Chapters I-XXXIX, p. 139):

>...The tendency of the ancient world to idealize the Ethiopian is familiar to the students of classical literature. To the Greeks they were the blameless Ethiopians (Homer), the tallest and handsomest of all men (Herodotus). Isaiah would seem to have been struck by the fine physique of the ambassadors, and perhaps it was their narrative that furnished his vivid imagination with the picturesque details crowded into these verses.

And oddly enough, Driver, in his book *Isaiah: His Life and Times*, pp. 91f., written in the 1880s inconsistent with his later views, wrote:

>By the ancients the character of the Ethiopians was almost idealized: they were imperfectly known to them, and yet report told that they controlled, in their distant home, an extensive empire. Homer applies to them the epithet "spotless," alluding to their physical beauty; and Herodotus calls them "the tallest and handsomest of men.... Ethiopia in

gratitude will own the power of Israel's God: and the ancient and mighty nation, in token of its faith, will send a "present"... to the place of the name... of Jehovah of hosts, the mount Zion.

Treatments of Moses' Cushite wife provide another example of racial myths governing Biblical interpretation. These treatments range all the way from viewing her as black, and thus despised by Miriam and Aaron, to her not having been black at all since, as the arguments go, she was a Midianite or an Asiatic Cushite which automatically made her white—or a second more recent wife than Zipporah.

Treatment of her as non-black goes back to rabbinical interpretation with its results shown in Midrashim and Gematria, and regards Cushite as having been used figuratively. It finds modern Jewish and Gentile expression in the New Hamite Myth that makes Asiatic Hamites-Cushites white. This latter view is contrary to evidence that Blacks inhabited lower Asia from most ancient times and were present even in Palestine within the Biblical period, as in the present; and that Blacks were present even within the Hebrew-Israelite-Judahite population at least from the time of the exodus from Egypt—even as they have been and are today among the Jews.

Older historians such as Maspero and Rawlinson claimed that the populations of Southern Asia included Negritos or little Negroes. Other writers such as H.G. Wells (*The Outline of History*, p. 134) and H.H. Johnston (*The Negro In The New World*, pp. 26f.) give extensive reports on Negroids in Asia. Emmanuel Anati (*Palestine Before The Hebrews*, p. 322) writes concerning "Negroid types" at Megiddo in Early Urban Palestine; and Chester C. McCown (*The Ladder of Progress In Palestine*, p. 166) discussed the necropolis at Beth-Shan which contained a woman with a broad flat nose. Further, McCown treats the inhabitants of Lachish as having been Upper Egyptian (p.143), even though Arthur Keith objected to the identification. And even in the Old Testament itself there is evidence supportive of a Black population within Palestine from Patriarchal times (Genesis 14) down to the time of Hezekiah (I Chronicles IV: 40f.). Even though most Jewish writers, from the time of the ancient rabbis onward, appear to have ignored or denied among the Hebrews and their offspring a Black presence, there are some who do include Negroes from the time of the Exodus. One who does so is Fritz Kahn, in his entry under RACE, JEWISH, *The Universal Jewish Encyclopedia*, Vol. 9, p.60. And Harry L.

Shapiro in his "Biological History of the Jewish People" (*Race and Science*, pp. 114ff.) admits of an Israelite Palestinian population suggestive of "negroid" affinities.

Interpretations of the superscription of Zephaniah (1:1) supply a broad spectrum of the association between racial myths and Biblical scholarship. In doing their interpretations scholars are faced with no fewer than three problems: the racial significance of the name "Cushi" given to the prophet's father; the identity of the Hezekiah referred to; and the relationship between Zephaniah's color-race-nationality and the Hezekiah named. Every conceivable answer has been given for the first two; only one scholar to my knowledge has dared to deal with the third.

Several scholars regard Cushi and consequently Zephaniah as having been Black/Ethiopian/"Negro" (as we have seen), as having been a slave, or at best of African origin, and thus unrelated blood-wise to a possible King Hezekiah of Judah. An equal number, disregarding a possible Black identify, make him a blood relative of the Hezekiah, whether king or not. Some among these latter in their discussion of the genealogy assert that it is given in order to make sure that there would be no identification of a black Zephaniah with a Judean. Thus George Fohrer in his *Introduction*, p. 456, writes, "It has been suggested that this (the genealogy) refers to the King of Judah who bore this name (Hezekiah). So that Zephaniah was of royal blood;... More likely, the ancestors of the father were named so as *to avoid the embarrassing misconception that Zephaniah's father, Cushi, was an Ethiopian and not a Judean.*" (Italics mine). So also Arthur Weiser in his *Introduction*, p. 264, and J.K. Kuntz in his *The People of Ancient Israel*, p. 315.

In response to assertions such as that made by Fohrer and the others, A.S. Kapelrud in his booklet *The Message of the Prophet Zephaniah*, p.44, quotes in French a comment made by C.S. Keller in his commentary on *Nahum, Habakkuk, Zephaniah*, p. 187. My shaky translation of Keller's comment is: "This explanation of the genealogy could only be born in the brain of an European obsessed with the problem of the races."

In view of the presence of Blacks within the Judahite population all along, some of whom were native born, there would seem to be no reason why Zephaniah could not be seen as a Black native Judahite, most likely related to Hezekiah, King of Judah. (See pictures of "Jesse Trees" in which one of the kings of Jesse's line is depicted black, and identified as Uzziah: Jean

Devisse and Michel Mollat, *The Image of the Black In Western Art*, 2, pp. 222 ff.

So-called racist interpretation by Biblical scholars reveals itself in a sin of omission rather than in a sin of commission in the case of Phinehas, grandson of Aaron (and in the case of his descendants also). And, strangely enough, the sin occurs in spite of the New Hamite Myth, and began to be indulged in at the very time that the myth was reaching its maturity among Biblical scholars.

At least since 1871 the name Phinehas has been interpreted to mean either Nubian or Negro, depending upon the racial attitude of the interpreter. (Here, again, however, Jewish scholars, in the main, object). Moreover, Albright, followed by many, in both his *From The Stone Age to Christianity*, pp. 193f., and in his *Yahweh and the Gods of Canaan*, p. 165, asserts that the presence of the name, derived from Egyptian Pi-Nehase, "The Nubian," indicates that there was a Nubian element in Moses's family. Writes Albright in the earlier book, "The name Phinehas, of which we have just spoken, is interesting as providing an independent (and absolutely reliable) confirmation of the tradition that there was a Nubian element in the family of Moses (Num. 12:1)."

That sin of omission, like the similar one in the case of Zephaniah, lies in the failure of Biblical scholars to follow up on the implications of their findings with respect to the racial affinities not only of Biblical Cushites but also of persons who were native members of the Hebrew community—and the significance of this for a more objective interpretation of the Bible—less mythical and freer of racist interpretation.

To be sure, one could deal with the several other passages in the Bible that contain references to Black people as has been done in the treatment of passages thus far. Additionally, one could give attention to such a name as Kedar, meaning "exceedingly black," with reference to the Kedarites referred to in the Bible, etc. The pressure of time precludes our doing so today.

So now, analyzing the interpretations of passages thus far dealt with, we note, aware of overlappings, what may be called categories of myths employed in some Biblical interpretation, as follows:

> A myth that all Blacks/Negroes, even in antiquity, were predominantly if not exclusively slaves;

A myth that Cushites-Nubians-Ethiopians-Negroes in antiquity were universally regarded with contempt;

A myth that the ancient Hebrew-Israelites-Judahites-Jews were all in physical appearance like Europeans, and exclusive of Blacks;

A myth that Cushites in Africa may be regarded as having been black, but not so those in Asia, or that black Cushites were non-existent in Asia;

A myth that Blacks/Negroes were far distant barbarians, unknown to the Hebrews and others until at best relatively later times.

And, related to them all is the New Hamite Myth—especially if one employs American definitions of Black/Negro.

Chapter 9

The Bible and
the African Experience:
The Biblical Period

In my opinion, the subject that has been announced for me to discuss, "The Bible and African Experience" is sufficiently broad to permit of, indeed to require, a division into several subtopics, each one of which merits serious consideration. It could well treat of the relationships between the Bible, viewed as a collection of writings that came into existence over a period of some twelve hundred years, and the continent of Africa from the time that the earliest of those writings were produced down to the present moment. For indeed Africa has a place in the biblical writings from the beginning, however far back in history one may set those beginnings.

What is more, Africa figures in the biblical history from the earliest times of creation when according to the biblical account four rivers went out from the Garden of Eden, one of which, the Gihon, went around the whole land of Cush or Ethiopia—a river that many view as the River Nile. Africa figures again in the earliest history in the account of the initial peopling of the earth as indicated in the Table of Nations (Genesis 10:6-10; 1 Chronicles 1:8-16) in which the eponymous ancestors of three African Nations or peoples (Cush/Ethiopia, Mizraim/Egypt, and Put(Phut)/Libya or Punt(Somaliland) and their offspring are referred to. And what is true of the earliest periods of history, as recorded in the Bible, is true of the biblical history in most of its periods into New Testament times.

Viewed from the perspective of the sixty-six books which make up the Protestant canon, Africa and some of her peoples appear in books that range from Genesis, in which are recorded the earliest biblical accounts, whether written by Moses or not, through chapter 7:9-10 of the Book of Revelation in which the Seer of Patmos envisions a host made up of peoples of every nation known to him, gathered before the throne of God. In fact, so prominently does Africa figure in some of the biblical content that one might well say. "No Africa, no biblical content."

On the other hand, not only does Africa and some of her peoples and places have a place within the biblical content, representing most periods of biblical history, but additionally, topic-wise, the Bible has had a place in the lives of African peoples ever since its existence as a body of sacred writings down to the present day. Even before that portion of the Bible known as the Hebrew Scriptures, the Old Testament of the Christians, had reached its final form around the year A.D. 100, Africans were acquainted with and using them, as is indicated by Luke's account of an Ethiopian eunuch who, as he was returning home to Africa from Jerusalem, was reading from the fifty-third chapter of the book of Isaiah. And, what is more, the eunuch was reading from a version of those Scriptures that had been produced in the African city of Alexandria, Egypt.

Such African use of the Bible continued and spread throughout North Africa and into what is known as both ancient and modern Ethiopia. In the meantime, Africans became foremost biblical scholars in interpreting and commenting upon the Bible. Alexandria became the center of a school of biblical interpretation.

When, after the passage of centuries, West Africans and their descendants were scattered around the world and introduced to the Bible, it became for many of them the book above all books.

Another topic of great importance has to do with not only how Africans viewed the Bible, but also with the ways in which they have understood, interpreted, and used it. Perhaps it is not too far off the subject to note that in numerous, but not in all instances, the interpretation of the Bible among West Africans and their dispersed relatives was influenced by their white enslavers, especially with reference to the so-called, un-biblical curse upon Ham and other passages that could be used to uphold the enslavement of Black peoples. And it is heartening to note that increasingly in more recent times, Black people in their continued use of the Bible are interpreting it from their own perspective. Thrilling is it, indeed, to note that they have moved from a position in which, in the year 1870, some requested the Pope to remove the curse of Ham from Black people[1] to a position from which today a Black Catholic priest in the Cameroon can unreservedly refer to the so-called curse of Ham as a *myth*[2] —even as many of those in the Diaspora have done at least since the late eighteenth century.

Certainly another possible sub-division of the general overall topic would have to treat of the African provenance of more or less goodly portions of the biblical content which must be attributed, directly and indirectly, to authors who were African—and this apart from their having been Hebrew-Israelite-Judahite, Jew. Furthermore, this authorship goes beyond the view that Moses, to whom the Pentateuch is attributed by some, was born and reared in Africa and thus was an African. Students of Africa might well pause, if only for a moment, to consider the traditions that the redactors of two of the Gospels, Mark and Matthew, carried out Apostolic ministries in Egypt and Ethiopia, respectively, and it would be interesting for such a study as this to note that the Apostle Paul, greatest of the contributors to the New Testament corpus, was on an occasion, accused of being an Egyptian revolutionist (Acts 21:38).

Sub-topics such as the foregoing do, indeed, merit development. Since time precludes such development, it will be left as a task for others, and the remainder of this essay will deal with the general subject only as it has to do with the Biblical Period.

Looking at Africa as part of the biblical content according to the Protestant Bible, it is to be observed that in addition to numerous instances in which reference is made to the mighty acts that God performed in Egypt on behalf of the Hebrews, the word "Egypt," along with cognates, and with allowances made for duplications of texts, occurs some 740 times in the Old Testament. The word "Ethiopia" and/or Cush, along with cognates, occurs fifty-eight times in the King James version of the Old Testament—*Ethiopia* thirty-nine times; *Cush* (untranslated), with cognates, nineteen times. And Put (Phut), identified as either Libya or Punt, occurs some seven times. In

----

1. This information comes from Claude Wauthier, *The Literature and Thought of Modern Africa: A Survey*, trans. Shirley Kay (New York: Praeger Publishers, 1967), p. 209.

2. E. Mveng, "La Bible et L'Afrique Noire," *The Jerusalem Congress On Black Africa and The Bible: Proceedings*, April 14-30, 1972, eds. E. Mveng and R.J.Z. Werblowsky (n.p.), p. 36.

the New Testament there are approximately fifty references to Africa and African personalities.

As anticipated previously, it is to be observed that the numerous references to Africa and Africans are located in several types of the biblical literature: in the Pentateuch or five books of the Law; in the so-called historical books; in the books of prophecy; in poetical-wisdom books—all in the Old Testament; and in the New Testament Gospels, the one historical book, letters, and the Apocalypse.

More specifically and in detail, the word "Egypt" occurs seventy-nine times in the accounts of the Hebrew patriarchs and Joseph; eighty-one times in the narratives of the Enslavement, Moses and the Exodus; one hundred and thirty five times with reference to the Hebrews having been brought out of Egypt. In eleven of the sixteen books of prophecy (including Daniel) reference is made to Egypt one hundred and eighty-three times; Jeremiah 62; Ezekiel 48; Isaiah 37; Hosea 13; Amos 7; Zachariah 5; Micah 4; Joel 1; Nahum 1; and Haggai 1. In the Old Testament historical books there are one and hundred eighteen references to Egypt, dealing with nine different events, while in the poetical-wisdom books Egypt is referred to six times.

With respect to Ethiopia, the country is referred to in the historical books in seven instances. And reference is made to it and its peoples in prophetic oracles within seven of the prophetical books, as follows: Isaiah 3; Jeremiah 3; Ezekiel 4; Daniel 1; Amos 1; Nahum 1; and Zephaniah 1. Three times the country is referred to in the poetical-wisdom literature.

Phut, or Put, appears five times in prophetical oracles within the books of Jeremiah, Ezekiel, and Nahum.

It is in assembling the numerous references to Africa and some of her peoples, and arranging them in the chronological sequence of biblical history, that we may view the African experience during the Biblical Period. This we shall now do according to the historical periods that follow. Before we engage in this enterprise, however, we must keep in mind the fact that in the Bible information about the African experience, in the main, is given by and from the perspective of Hebrew-Israelite-Judahite-Jewish writers—not by nor from the viewpoint of Africans, except where it can be established that Africans, whether Hebrew or otherwise, were the authors. Africans, so to speak, are passive providers of the information in most instances.

With this awareness, we may proceed to deal with the African experience according to the following eight historical periods: 1) The Period of the Patriarchs and Joseph; 2) The

Period of the Enslavement, Exodus, and Wilderness Wanderings; 3) The Period of the Judges; 4) The Period of the United Monarchy; 5) The Period of the Two Kingdoms—Israel and Judah; 6) The Period of One Kingdom—Judah; 7) The Period of the Exile and Restoration; and 8) The New Testament Period.

The Period Of The Patriarchs And Joseph

During the period of the patriarchs and Joseph the African Experience in relation to the Bible is set forth in the narratives about Abraham, father of the Hebrews; of Jacob, father of the Israelites; and of Joseph, father of the two most important northern tribes of Israel, as will be noted again further along—all within the book of Genesis. In the instance of Isaac, it is expressly stated that he must not go down to Egypt (Genesis 26:2). Relative to Abraham it is recounted that because of famine in the land of Canaan he and his entourage, including Lot who was to become the father of the Ammonites and Moabites, migrated to Egypt. There they remained until the pharaoh expelled them but not before bestowing upon Abraham great riches. It is further recounted that in Egypt Abraham obtained an Egyptian maid, Hagar, by whom he sired his first-born son, Ishmael. For Ishmael, his mother obtained an Egyptian wife. In turn, Ishmael became the father of several progeny among whom was Kedar, the exceedingly black one, who became ancestor of several tribes in Asia.

Part and parcel of the narratives concerning Jacob is that which recounts the selling of Jacob's favorite son, Joseph, into Egypt, where he has several experiences including being elevated to a position of power second only to that of the pharaoh himself, and his receiving in marriage an Egyptian wife. In the meantime, Jacob, as the account continues, finds it necessary to send some of his sons to Egypt in order to purchase food during a time of famine in Canaan. A climax is reached in the narrative when Jacob, with his entire family moves to Egypt where they are given residence in the region of Goshen; and the story ends with Jacob's death and burial in the land of Canaan whither his sons carry the corpse, accompanied by Egyptians who join in the mourning.

Returning to the accounts concerning Joseph: he sires two sons by his Egyptian wife, Asenath, Ephraim and Manasseh, who as noted, become the fathers of the two chief northern tribes in the land of Canaan. When he dies his body is embalmed and kept unburied in anticipation of the time when the Hebrews return to the land promised to their fathers.

Thus during the period of the patriarchs and Joseph, Africa figures prominently in the life of the Hebrews in a mutually wholesome and satisfactory manner, with the blood of Hebrews and Egyptians becoming mixed, at least among important persons of the two groups. Two of the most important so-called twelve tribes of Israel will not only have had their origin in Egypt in Africa, but will be half-Egyptian through their mother.

Somewhat incidental to the African Experience, in view of the fact that Egypt in the Bible is referred to as the land or tents of Ham (Psalms 78:51, 105:23,27, 106:21ff.) is a reference to a land of Ham in the vicinity of Canaan during the time of the patriarch Abraham (Genesis 14), and yet a second reference to the children of Ham as occupants of a Canaanite region until the time of King Hezekiah (I Chronicles 4:40 ff.).

The Period of the Enslavement, Exodus, and The Wilderness Wanderings

According to the biblical account, the African Experience was the only experience known to the Hebrews for a period of some four hundred years. During this time they are depicted as living not only in the land of Goshen, but also as living side by side with Egyptians. In the course of time, several years after the death of Joseph, when a pharaoh who knew nothing of Joseph, ascended the throne fearful that the Hebrews, now becoming numerous, might become a national security risk, the Hebrews were enslaved and a policy of genocide instituted against them. In this state of enslavement they remained until, under the leadership of Moses, and after a series of plagues inflicted by God upon the Egyptians, they escaped from Egypt across the Sea of Reeds into the desert, in the event known as the Exodus. Sharing with Hebrews in the event was a mixed multitude which, as Leviticus 24:10ff. recounts, included Egyptians.

Important, indeed, is it to note that in their going out from Egypt the Hebrews and fellow travelers were not paupers. The latter chapters of the book of Exodus, and other passages indicate that they went out not only equipped for war, but also possessing great wealth.

But the African Experience during the period of the Enslavement and Exodus is not exhausted in the general, overall picture just depicted. The biblical record provides evidence at several points, in addition to the reference to a mixed multitude, that the African Experience was one and the same or was identical with the Hebrew Experience. Africans constituted at least some elements among the Hebrews—apart from the fact that all Hebrews living in Egypt across the centuries were Africans by birth. Particularly is this so in the case of Moses and his family. One may note that Moses is not identified as a Hebrew, but as an Egyptian by the daughters of Jethro (Exodus 2:19), which identity (as later rabbis were to note) Moses did not deny.[3] Further, many names in the family of Moses, such as the name Moses itself, Aaron, Mirari, Miriam, Putiel, Hophni, and Phinehas are Egyptian names. The name of Phinehas, grandson of Aaron, means the Nubian or Negro, depending upon the given translator. This is indicative, according to scholars of note, that the whole family of Moses was of African/Nubian/Negro origin.[4] And, it may be added, that from ancient Greek and Roman times until the present, by some Jews as well as Gentiles, Moses and even the Hebrew people as a whole, have been believed to have been of either Egyptian or Ethiopian provenance.[5] Added to all this is the account of Moses' having married a Cushite/Ethiopian wife who if Zipporah, a daughter of the Midianite-Kenite priest, reflects Africa in Asia once again, as in the case of Ishmael and his descendants; or if not Zipporah, then, as Josephus and some rabbinic midrashim would have it, the daughter of a king of Ethiopia.[6]

The African Experience is reflected once again in the influence of Africa upon the Hebrews, especially during the period of the sojourn in Egypt, the period which saw Israel come into being as a people. And increasingly, scholars of differing theological persuasions are recognizing and admitting African origin and influence upon much of what appears in the biblical

---

3. See Louis Ginzberg, *Legends of the Bible* (New York: Simon and Schuster, 1956), p.305.

4. William Foxwel Albright in *From The Stone Age to Christianity.* (Baltimore: The John Hopkins Press, 1946), p. 193ff., and *Yahweh and The Gods of Canaan* (Garden City, New York: Doubleday & Company, Inc., 1969), p. 165.

5. For discussions of the Egyptian and/or Ethiopian origin of Moses, and of the Jews, see Sigmund Freud, *Moses and Monotheism*, trans. Katherine Jones (New York: Vintage Books, 1939); John G. Gager, *Moses in Greco-Roman Paganism* (Nashville: Abingdon Press, 1972); Flavius Jospehus, *Antiquities of the Jews*, 5, 2, trans. William Whiston in *The Works of Flavius Jospehus* (Hartford, Conn.: S.C. Scranton Co., 1903), 923, and Elias Auerbach, *Moses*, trans. and eds. Robert A. Barclay and Israel O. Lehman (Detroit: Wayne State University Press, 1975).

6. Josephus, op.cit., 2, 10; Ginzberg, op. cit., pp. 300ff., by way of examples.

content, beginning with Moses and his time and continuing across the centuries. This is to say that some of the biblical content itself, as well as Hebrew culture referred to in the Bible, is of direct African derivation, or based upon African culture. Estimates of the extent of origin and influence vary among scholars, and it is most interesting to note that the conservative scholar Charles F. Aling in his book *Egypt and Bible History From Earliest Times* to 1000 B.C., asserts that Israel owes a great debt to Egypt.[7] Among things that he considers borrowed by the Hebrews from the Egyptians are linguistic borrowing; proper names; wisdom literature such as Proverbs 22:17-23:14; social and political institutions such as governmental structure by Solomon; scribal schools in Jerusalem to train young men for government service; titles found in the Israelite bureaucracy going back to the time of David, etc. Another scholar, Marcel Laperrugue of France, whose views are set forth in an essay entitled, "The Bible and the Civilizations of the Nile Valley" (my English translation) published in the book *Black Africa and the Bible*, lists and discusses as borrowings the rite of circumcision, worship of the golden calf, the solar cult, the cult of trees, worship on high places, and the temple of Solomon—to name a few.[8] And with this latter listing of things borrowed from the Egyptians by the Hebrews the prophet Ezekiel would be in substantial agreement at many points, for in castigating Judah for her sins he states, "Thus will I make thy lewdness to cease from thee, and thy whoredom brought from the land of Egypt: so that thou should not lift up thine eyes unto them, nor remember Egypt any more (Ezekiel 23:27).

The Period of the Judges

The Bible records hardly anything of an African Experience during the period of the Judges, that period between the entrance of the former Hebrew slaves into the land of Canaan under the leadership of Joshua and the establishment of a monarchy under Saul. However, one thing to be noted is the continuing function of the African-based Aaronic priesthood through such persons as Eli and his two sons, both of whom bear the Egyptian names Hophni and Phinehas. A second item is that

---

7. Op. cit. (Grand Rapids, Mich.: Baker Book House, 1981), pp. 123ff.

8. Op. cit., pp. 173ff.

Egyptians, as distinct from Hebrews, continue to make up part of the population and that there is intermarriage between the two groups as is attested in the account of the Hebrew Sheshan's giving one of his daughters in marriage to an Egyptian slave (I Chronicles 2:34).

The Period of the United Monarchy

The period of the United Monarchy, during which Saul, David, and Solomon reigned, and which lasted roughly from 1028 to 922 B.C., is one that witnessed increasing relations between Hebrew-Israelites-Judahites in Canaan and Africans, especially during the reign of Solomon.

A Black soldier, referred to only as the Cushite, appears as a member of David's private army in the account of Absalom's revolt (II Samuel 18). He could have been an ordinary Black Israelite-Judahite, or a member of a Philistine contingent from Crete, an island inhabited from earliest times by peoples from Africa.[9] Toward the end of David's reign Hadad of Edom fled to Egypt for asylum after an unsuccessful revolt, and remained there until after David's death (I Kings 11:17ff.). In the meantime the reigning pharaoh gave to Hadad an Egyptian wife, sister to the queen.

At several points the African Experience enters the records of Solomon's reign. First and foremost, perhaps, Solomon's chief wife was an Egyptian princess whose father captured and gave to Solomon the city of Gezer as a dowry; and whom an early Church Father identified with the Black Maiden in the Song of Songs.[10] Then there are the accounts of Solomon's trade with Egypt, and with Ophir which is identified by some as a location in Africa (I Kings 10:28ff.; I Kings 9:26-28). Further, there is the account of the visit by the Queen of Sheba whose kingdom, as it appears, included parts of Africa as well as territory in southwest Arabia (I Kings 10:1-13; II Chronicles 9:1-12). Additionally there are the accounts of Hadad's return from Egypt upon the death of David, and of Jeroboam's finding refuge in Egypt after escaping the wrath of

---

9. Scholarly opinion today recognizes this to be an uncontested fact.

10. See Robert M. Grant, *The Bible in the Church: A Short History of Interpretation* (New York: Macmillan Co., 1948), pp. 77ff.

Solomon, remaining there until Solomon's death (I Kings 11:14-22,40).

The Period of the Two Kingdoms Israel and Judah 922 B.C. —722 B.C.

The African Experience, so prominent during the reign of Solomon continued to be outstanding after his death through the succeeding generations. Hardly had the United Monarchy split into two kingdoms when Sheshonk I, pharaoh of Egypt, called Shishak in the Bible, invaded Judah the southern kingdom, and depleted it of its wealth, in addition to reducing the kingdom to vassalage.

The account given in I Kings 14-25-28 is duplicated and expanded both historically and theologically by the author of II Chronicles (12:2-12). According to the Chronicler, Shishak invaded the country with twelve hundred chariots and sixty thousand horsemen. His army, so large as to be innumerable, included Egyptians, Libyans, Sukkim, and Ethiopians. And still further, according to the Chronicler, Judah was invaded a second time during the reign of King Asa by Zerah the Ethiopian, whose army numbered a million men. On this second occasion the invaders are reported to have been defeated by God and completely destroyed (II Chronicles 14:9-15). Just who this Zerah, the Ethiopian, was cannot be agreed upon by historians. Some regard him as an Arab chieftain, while others think that he may have been head of an occupation force left in the land by Shishak.[11]

During the eighth century, Africa enters the picture once again shortly before the fall of the northern kingdom in 721 B.C. Second Kings 17:4 reports that Hoshea, last king of Israel, sought aid from So, king of Egypt, in his revolt against Shalmaneser, King of Assyria. The prophet Hosea criticizes Israel for such activity (Hosea 7:11-16); prophesies that Israel shall return to Egypt (Hosea 9:3,6); takes note that God had called Israel, His son, out of the land of Egypt (Hosea 11:1); and has been Israel's God since the days of Egypt (Hosea 11:9). Some commentators interpret Hosea 7:11 and 9:16 to mean that during the closing years of the northern kingdom many Israelites

----

11. See John Bright, *A History of Israel*, 3rd ed. (Philadelphia: Westminster Press, 1981), p. 234ff.

abandoned their homeland and settled in Egypt, as later many of the inhabitants of Judah would do.[12]

Shortly before Hosea had uttered his prophecies, the prophet Amos had had occasion to make reference to the Ethiopians, saying that they were equal to the people of Israel in the sight of God (Amos 9:7).

The Period of the One Kingdom—Judah

It is in the book of Isaiah and corresponding passages in II Kings and II Chronicles that the African Experience during the last days of Israel and the next immediate generation in Judah is recounted. This next immediate generation is the hey-day of the twenty-fifth Ethiopian/Egyptian dynasty which ruled over both Egypt and Ethiopia, and struggled with the Assyrians for dominance in Western Asia. Ethiopia/Egypt entered the picture as allies of Hezekiah, King of Judah, under the leadership of Tirhakah who later was to become pharaoh (II Kings 19:9; Isaiah 37:9). Judah's reliance upon Ethiopia/Egypt instead of upon God during these days is most severely rebuked by the prophet Isaiah who, in verbal and symbolic prophecies, condemns Judah's action in this regard. In Chapter 18 of the Book of Isaiah is the prophet's address to the ambassadors of the Ethiopians, a people whom he describes as "a nation tall and smooth, a people feared near and far, a nation mighty and conquering, whose land the rivers divide" (18:1-2 RSV). And in Chapter 19 appears a strange oracle concerning Egypt that may come from a later time. The oracle vacillates between pronouncing doom upon and the restoration of Egypt, and predicts a time when the Egyptians will be co-worshipers of God with Assyrians and Israelites. Chapter 20 depicts the prophet as going about as a captive of war over a period of three years, symbolic of the doom that it is to come upon the Egyptians and Ethiopians. And the prophet's rebuke is continued in Chapters 30 and 31 of the book in which he proclaims woe upon Judah for her trust in Egypt. At the same time he depicts the military might of the African kingdom. He declares:

> Woe to them that go down to Egypt for help; and
> stay on horses, and trust in chariots, because they

---

12. The Judahite flight to Egypt is recorded in II Kings 25:26, and in Jeremiah 43:1-7.

are many; and in horsemen, because they are very strong; but they look not unto the Holy One of Israel, neither seek the Lord!...Now the Egyptians are men, and not God; and their horses flesh and not spirit.... (Isaiah 31:1, 3).

For the next seventy-five years after the prophet Isaiah the African Experience finds no reflection in the Scriptures, except that given in retrospect to the fall of Thebes in 663 B.C. by the prophet Nahum. Beginning around 626 B.C., however, the experience reenters the Bible in the form of historical narratives, prophetic oracles, and accounts pertaining to some persons who were of both direct and indirect African descent.

To begin with, there is the person of and the oracles of the prophet Zephaniah. Zephaniah's father is stated to have been one Cushi(Zephaniah 1:1)—the Cushite/Ethiopian/Negro. His family tree is traced back to one Hezekiah, thought by some to have been none other than the king of Judah. The prophet's identity is a much disputed matter among the scholars. It may be noted that one school of thought views him as a native Black African who was active as a prophet in Judah.[13] Another regards him as a Black Judahite who most likely was a member of the royal family.[14] And there is, to be sure, a third opinion that thinks that despite his father's name, "Cushi," he was neither Black nor related to the king.[15] Whatever his color and his relationship to Africa, the African Experience finds reference in his prophecies. On one hand he pronounces doom upon the Ethiopians who still in his day are an outstanding people (Zephaniah 2:12), while on the other hand he predicts a day when worshipers of Yahweh will come from beyond the rivers of Ethiopia and bring offerings (Zephaniah 3:9-10). The context of the latter prophecy indicates that these worshipers are not to be people dispersed from Judah but native Africans. Thus the passage is akin to Psalm 68:31 which portrays Ethiopia as stretching out her hands to God.

----

13. This view is supported by Gene Rice in his article, "The African Roots of the Prophet Zephaniah," *The Journal of Religious Thought*, 36, (Spring-Summer, 1979): 21-31.

14. This is the opinion of the writer.

15. A survey of Old Testament "Introductions" establishes this view as the majority one among white scholars, except that when the prophet is viewed as having been Black he is assumed to have been a slave.

Hardly had the voice of Zephaniah ceased from speaking before the prophet Nahum predicted the fall of Nineveh, capital of the Assyrian empire. In doing so he compared Nineveh's forthcoming destruction with that of Thebes, capital of the great Egyptian empire, fifty years previously. In a bold question he asks Assyria's capital city, "Art thou better than populous No (Thebes) that was situate among the rivers, that had the waters round about it, whose rampart was the sea, and her wall was from the sea?" He then goes on to say that Thebes fell despite the fact that she was aided by Ethiopia, Egypt, Put, and the Lubim (Nahum 3:8-9).

Shortly after the time of Nahum, the African Experience, with respect to historical events, is depicted in the Books of II Kings, II Chronicles, and Jeremiah. Second Kings 23:29-24:5, duplicated and expanded on II Chronicles 35:20-36:4, recounts Egypt's domination of Judah during the period 609-605 B.C., under Pharaoh Necho, specifying Necho's defeat of King Josiah, the dethronement and deportation of King Jehoahaz to Egypt, and the Egyptian installation of Jehoiakim as king of Judah. During Jehoiakim's reign, according to Jeremiah 26:20-23, Uriah, a prophet, who like Jeremiah had prophesied against Jerusalem and Judah, escaped for safety to Egypt, only to be brought back and executed by the king.

As a book, Jeremiah alone is a treasure trove of references to the African Experience. As previously stated, it contains 62 references to Egypt as a country, apart from references to Ethiopia and other African lands. In addition to historical events recorded in the book, some of which have already been mentioned, there are several oracles against Judah's seeking Egypt's help; oracles of doom upon Egypt; oracles of doom upon Judahites some of whom remain in Judah and some of whom have fled to Egypt, and delivered in Egypt; and one brief oracle that is favorably disposed toward Egypt.

Moreover, the book contains historical accounts about persons of both immediate and remote African descent. Included in the remote category is the person of Jehudi, great-grandson of one Cushi, and obviously a court official, who read Jeremiah's scroll of prophecies in the presence of King Jehoiakim only to have the scroll cut in pieces and thrown into the fire (Jeremiah 36:14-23). Similarly there are the accounts about Ebed-melech the Ethiopian, another official in the Judahite court, who was instrumental in saving Jeremiah's life, and was afterwards blessed by the prophet (Jeremiah 38:7-13; 39:15-18). Prior to these accounts there is Jeremiah's impartial analogy between Judah's inability to alter her wicked ways and the Ethiopian's powerlessness to change the color of his skin (Jeremiah 13:23). And in chapters 40:1-43:8, which is an expansion of what is recorded in II Kings 25:26, there is an account of a group of Judahites who fled to Egypt, taking the prophet Jeremiah with them against his will.

The Period of the Exile and Restoration

The later references to the African Experience in the book of Jeremiah are to be dated in the period of the Exile; while references in the Book of Ezekiel make for an overlap between the last days of Judah and the Exile, and the references in Ezekiel are second in number only to those in Jeremiah. It is to be observed that with the exception of three verses in Ezekiel 29:16-18, which predict a restoration of Egypt, and Egypt's recognition of Yahweh as Lord, all of Chapters 29-32 consist of prophecies that in one way or another are antagonistic toward Egypt. Even so, Ezekiel's anti-Egyptian oracles show her to be, at least in his opinion, a proud, great, wealthy nation, ruler over nations among whom she stands as a lion, exerting great influence upon both Hebrew kingdoms, not only in times past but even in his own day—almost a hundred years after the fall of Thebes to the Assyrians in 663 B.C. It is not without historical interest to note that according to Ezekiel, Egypt's origins lay in the land of Pathros, Upper Egypt, and that it is there that she will be restored, albeit as a lowly kingdom. But Egypt is not to be alone in her forthcoming destruction: her African allies, especially Ethiopia, then Put, Lud, and Libya; and Asiatic Arabia are to go down with her (Ezekiel 30:1-9).

Dating from the period of the Restoration is Isaiah 27:13-23 in which a prophet foresees a return of exiles from Egypt and Assyria to Jerusalem in order to worship on the holy mountain. And belonging also to this period, as providing data on the African Experience, are passages in that portion of the Book of Isaiah referred to as the Second Isaiah, chapters 40-55. Additionally, and indicative of that experience, are Psalms such as 78:51, with its reference to the "tents of Ham"; and Psalms 105:23-27, and 106:21f., with their references to Egypt as the "land of Ham," the two latter dating from after the fall of Jerusalem in 586 B.C., as their contexts indicate. Perhaps also in the post-Exilic period belongs Psalm 68 with its verse 31 in which it is said that princes shall come out of Egypt, and Ethiopia shall soon stretch out hands unto God.

The data in Second Isaiah consist of Chapters 43:3 and 45:14. In speaking of Judah's restoration the prophet asserts that Yahweh will ransom Israel by exchanging Egypt and Ethiopia for her, and that the wealth of Egypt and the merchandise of Ethiopia, along with the Sabeans, will become Israel's possession, even as slaves, and will acknowledge Israel's God.

Of the five references to Egypt in the Book of Zechariah, dated between 332-164 B.C., one prophesies that Jewish exiles will be brought back to Palestine from the land of Egypt (10:10-11), while a second (14:18-19) states, strangely, that a plague will come upon the Egyptians if they fail to come up to Jerusalem in order to observe the Feast of Booths.

The New Testament Period

The African Experience is reflected in the New Testament in only a few instances. Passages that do reflect it appear twice in the Gospel according to Matthew, one instance each in Mark and Luke, duplicating one of the passages in Matthew; and five or six times in the book of Acts. Two indirect references appear in the Book of Revelation.

Matthew 2:13ff. recounts Joseph's flight with Mary and the infant Jesus into Egypt where, as his people across the centuries before him, he found refuge and remained until after the death of Herod. Also in Matthew 27:26, as in Mark 15:21 and Luke 23:26, is the account of Simon of Cyrene who was forced to help Jesus carry the cross. Acts 2:5-10 records that on the Day of Pentecost there were present in Jerusalem both Jews and proselytes from Egypt and parts of Libya belonging to Cyrene; and Chapter 6:9 states that Cyrenians and Alexandrians were among those who disputed with Stephen.

Additionally in Acts, there is Stephen's long speech in the course of which he reviews the history of his people, including their enslavement in Egypt (7:2-37); and a similar speech delivered by Paul in Antioch of Pisidia (13:16ff.). Prior to Paul's speech, chronologically, is the narrative of Phillip's conversion of an Ethiopian eunuch who was reading from the Book of Isaiah, and who obviously was a proselyte or God-Fearer. Acts 13:1 states that among the prophets and teachers at Antioch in Syria was one Simeon called the Black One, and Lucious of Cyrene. Somewhat like the surveys of their people's history by Stephen and Paul are passages in the Book of Hebrews which refer to Moses and the event of the Exodus (3:16; 8:9; 11:20ff.).

Revelation 7:9-10 and 14:6ff.[16] serve well to conclude New Testament passages that reflect the African Experience. The first reads:

> After this I looked, and behold, a great multitude which no man could number, from every nation, from all tribes and peoples and tongues, standing before the throne and before the Lamb, clothed in white robes, with palm branches in their hands, and crying with a loud voice "Salvation belongs to our God who sits upon the throne and the Lamb."

And the second reads:

> Then I saw another angel flying in midheaven, with an eternal gospel to proclaim to those who dwell on earth, to every nation and tribe and tongue and people; and he said with a loud voice "Fear God and give him Glory, for the hour of His judgment has come; and worship Him who made heaven and earth, the sea and the fountains of water."

CONCLUSION

Thus, to say nothing about the several subdivisions into which the general subject may be divided, that one which is limited to the African Experience during the biblical period alone reveals that the experience is present in several ways. It is present in the literature of many of the periods of biblical history, and in almost every type of the literature. Africa figures as home and place of refuge from the time of Abraham through the time of Jesus. Africans, from slaves to rulers, appear as actors on the stage of history. Authors of much of the biblical content were native Africans in origin. And in the veins of Hebrew-Israelites-Judahites-Jewish peoples flowed African blood. Indeed, in numerous instances, the biblical experience is an African Experience.

----
16. Read in the Revised Standard Version.

BLACK LIGHT FELLOWSHIP

Resources on Black people in Biblical history and experience.

The Black Presence in the Bible *(Vol. 1, Teacher's Guide)*
Discovering the Black and African Identity of Biblical
Persons and Nations (1990) Rev. Walter Arthur McCray
ISBN: 0-933176-12-0 $19.95

**The Black Presence in the Bible and the Table of Nations
(Genesis 10:1-32)** *(Vol. 2, Table of Nations)*
With emphasis on the Hamitic Genealogical Line from a
Black Perspective (1990) Rev. Walter Arthur McCray
ISBN: 0-933176-13-9 $19.95

Black Biblical Studies: An Anthology of Charles B. Copher
Biblical and Theological Issues on The Black Presence in
the Bible (1993) Charles B. Copher
ISBN: 0-933176-38-4 $14.95

BLACK LIGHT FELLOWSHIP
P.O. Box 5369 · Chicago, IL 60680
312.563.0081

CHARLES B. COPHER

The Reverend Dr. Charles B. Copher is a distinguished and eminent scholar of the Old Testament, and minister of the Gospel of Jesus Christ in the United Methodist Church. Formerly Vice President for Academic Affairs and Dean of the Faculty, he now serves as Professor Emeritus and Adjunct Professor of Old Testament at the Interdenominational Theological Center in Atlanta, Georgia, lecturing in ancient Black Biblical history. He and his wife *Marie* reside in the Adamsville community of Atlanta.

Copher's educational and theological credentials include a B.A. from Clark College, a M.Div. from Gammon Theological Seminary, a B.D. from Oberlin Graduate School of Theology, and the Ph.D. in Biblical Literature from Boston University. His writings have appeared in numerous textbooks, religious publications, and journals across the nation, and he is a contributing author to the *Encyclopedia Britannica.* During the second semester of the 1987-1988 school year, **Copher** served as *Distinguished Visiting Professor* at the Howard University School of Divinity.

Widely respected in academic, Christian, and community circles, **Copher** is sought across the nation for his in-depth Biblical, theological, historical, and educational lectures. He is at once intellectually incisive, reverentially spiritual, genuinely humble, and emotionally stimulating.

Black Biblical Studies is **Copher's** first book in Black studies, and serves as a major contribution toward understanding the Bible's Black and African presence. The community eagerly awaits what is expected to be an epochal work from the hand of **Copher**: a major book entitled *Black Peoples and Personalities In and From the Bible.*